Film Lover's PARIS

237412

BARBARA BOESPFLUG
BEATRICE BILLON

PHOTOS: PIERRE-OLIVIER SIGNE
ART DIRECTION: STANISLAS POTIÉ

PREFACE

This guide, which we hope is new and original, presents a selection of favourite places tha offer a unique connection with films we love: discover the decors, relive the scenes, feel th emotions and, finally, understand why the directors chose to film in these wonderful places The idea for this book germinated for a year, during which time we looked at it from al sorts of complex and bizarre angles, and even around the world. But Paris quite naturall brought its own dimension to the project with its repertoire of fabulous places drawn fron the birthplace of cinema. It remained then only to go and discover them. Of course, som places wouldn't allow us access and others had changed so much that they were no longer o interest, but our enthusiasm outweighed our disappointment and led us to these 101 iconi places, whose drama is accessible to all.

To help you find your way around, the guide is organised by area and includes practica information for each place, such as the number of stars indicating the price: one sta corresponds to around 10€, except for hotels, where it equates to 100€. Finally, the Q codes enable you to access trailers or information about the films.

We hope that the book you're holding in your hands will prove worthy of the passion w put into creating it.

Beatrice & Barbara

PS: The guide is based on our visits, and the information it contains was obtained, at the time of writing, from document newspaper articles, interviews and via other resourceful means. Unfortunately, it is therefore possible that, despite all ou precautions and scrupulous checking, some information may be out of date or incorrect by the time you discover these places.

CONTENTS

◼ HÔTEL DE VILLE/MARAIS
Page 6

01 L'HÔTEL DE SOUBISE • *MARIE-ANTOINETTE* — *Page 8*
02 L'HÔTEL DE ROHAN • *'QUARTIER DES ENFANTS ROUGES' – PARIS, I LOVE YOU* — *Page 10*
03 LE GEORGES • *THE STORY OF MY LIFE* — *Page 12*
04 L'ÉTOILE MANQUANTE • *A HAPPY EVENT* — *Page 14*
05 L'ANNEXE • *POLISSE* — *Page 15*
06 PAUL • *MIDNIGHT IN PARIS* — *Page 16*
07 KONG • *TELL NO ONE* — *Page 18*

◼ TUILERIES/PALAIS-ROYAL
Page 20

08 MAXIM'S • *CHÉRI* — *Page 22*
09 L'HÔTEL COSTES • *THE ACTRESS' BALL* — *Page 25*
10 LE MEURICE • *W.E.* — *Page 26*
11 ANGELINA • *LA BOUM 2* — *Page 28*
12 HÔTEL SAINT JAMES & ALBANY SPA • *THE BEAT THAT MY HEART SKIPPED* — *Page 30*
13 L'HÔTEL REGINA • *THE BOURNE IDENTITY* — *Page 33*
14 THE DEFENDER • *THE CORSICAN FILE* — *Page 34*
15 LE NEMOURS • *THE TOURIST* — *Page 36*
16 VILLALYS • *PARIS* — *Page 38*
17 LE GRAND VÉFOUR • *COCO BEFORE CHANEL* — *Page 40*
18 LE GRAND COLBERT • *SOMETHING'S GOTTA GIVE* — *Page 43*
19 LA GALERIE DORÉE DE LA BANQUE DE FRANCE • *VATEL* — *Page 44*
20 LEGRAND FILLES & FILS • *ROMANTICS ANONYMOUS* — *Page 46*

◼ ÉTOILE/CHAMPS-ÉLYSÉES
Page 48

21 LE BRISTOL • *MIDNIGHT IN PARIS* — *Page 50*
22 CLUB 13 • *L'AVENTURE, C'EST L'AVENTURE* — *Page 53*
23 CINÉMA MAC MAHON • *BREATHLESS* — *Page 54*
24 TUTTI FIESTA • *L'AMOUR C'EST MIEUX À DEUX* — *Page 56*
25 LE CENTRE DE TIR DE PARIS DE LA POLICE NATIONALE • *LA FEMME NIKITA* — *Page 58*
26 L'HÔTEL RAPHAEL • *HOTEL CHEVALIER* — *Page 60*
27 PERSHING HALL • *LITTLE WHITE LIES* — *Page 62*
28 LE MUSÉE GALLIERA • *THE DEVIL WEARS PRADA* — *Page 64*
29 LE TOKYO EAT • *HUNTING AND GATHERING* — *Page 66*
30 LA MAISON BLANCHE • *AVENUE MONTAIGNE* — *Page 68*
31 LE PLAZA ATHÉNÉE • *AVENUE MONTAIGNE* — *Page 71*
32 LES OMBRES • *CHANGE OF PLANS* — *Page 72*
33 LA TOUR EIFFEL • *A VIEW TO A KILL* — *Page 74*
34 MATSURI • *THE BIG PICTURE* — *Page 76*

■ SAINT-DENIS/SAINT-MARTIN   *Page 78*

35 L'AUBERGE PYRÉNÉES CÉVENNES • *OSS 117: CAIRO, NEST OF SPIES*   *Page 80*
36 L'HÔTEL DU NORD• *HOTEL DU NORD*   *Page 83*
37 L'ATMOSPHÈRE • *RUSSIAN DOLLS*   *Page 84*
38 POINT ÉPHÉMÈRE *'LOLITA' – THE PLAYERS*   *Page 86*
39 L'HÔTEL KUNTZ • *BELOVED*   *Page 88*
40 LE BRADY • *LOVE SONGS*   *Page 89*
41 LE PASSAGE BRADY • *FRANTIC*   *Page 91*
42 JULIEN • *LA VIE EN ROSE*   *Page 92*

■ BELLEVILLE   *Page 94*

43 LE MÉCANO BAR • *LITTLE WHITE LIES*   *Page 97*
44 AUX FOLIES • *PARIS*   *Page 98*
45 LE ZÉPHYR • *CHANGE OF PLANS*   *Page 101*
46 LA HALLE AUX OLIVIERS • *CHANGE OF PLANS*   *Page 102*

■ BASTILLE   *Page 104*

47 LE PETIT BOFINGER • *THE CONCERT*   *Page 106*
48 L' ENTRE POTES • *WHEN THE CAT'S AWAY*   *Page 108*
49 LE PAUSE CAFÉ • *WHEN THE CAT'S AWAY*   *Page 113*
50 LE PURE CAFÉ • *BEFORE SUNSET*   *Page 114*
51 AU VIEUX CHÊNE • *I'VE BEEN WAITING SO LONG*   *Page 116*
52 LE SQUARE TROUSSEAU • *LE PÈRE NOËL EST UNE ORDURE*   *Page 118*
53 LE MARCHÉ D'ALIGRE • *'BASTILLE' – PARIS, I LOVE YOU*   *Page 121*
54 LE TRAIN BLEU • *LA FEMME NIKITA*   *Page 122*

■ MONTMARTRE   *Page 124*

55 AU MARCHÉ DE LA BUTTE • *AMÉLIE*   *Page 126*
56 LE MANÈGE DU SACRÉ-CŒUR • *ITINÉRAIRE D'UN ENFANT GÂTÉ*   *Page 128*
57 LE FUNICULAIRE DE MONTMARTRE • *A MONSTER IN PARIS*   *Page 129*
58 STUDIO 28 • *AMÉLIE*   *Page 130*
59 LE CAFÉ DES 2 MOULINS • *AMÉLIE*   *Page 133*
60 LE MOULIN ROUGE • *MOULIN ROUGE!*   *Page 134*
61 LA BOULANGERIE DU MOULIN DE LA GALETTE • *JULIE & JULIA*   *Page 135*
62 LA RENAISSANCE • *INGLOURIOUS BASTERDS*   *Page 137*
63 TIN-TIN TATOUEUR • *DÉPRESSION ET DES POTES*   *Page 138*
64 LE CERCLE CLICHY MONTMARTRE • *BELOVED*   *Page 141*
65 L'HÔTEL CAMELIA • *TAKEN*   *Page 142*

OPÉRA/TRINITÉ
Page 144

66 LE RESTAURANT AMOUR • *LOVE LASTS THREE YEARS*   *Page 146*
67 LE FOLIE'S CAFÉ • *MENSCH*   *Page 148*
68 À LA MÈRE DE FAMILLE • *ROMANTICS ANONYMOUS*   *Page 150*
69 LE BOUILLON CHARTIER • *A VERY LONG ENGAGEMENT*   *Page 153*
70 ATHÉNÉE THÉÂTRE LOUIS-JOUVET • *HUGO*   *Page 154*
71 SENDERENS • *HEREAFTER*   *Page 156*

SAINT-GERMAIN/INVALIDES
Page 158

72 LE MUSÉE RODIN • *MIDNIGHT IN PARIS*   *Page 160*
73 L'HÔTEL D'AVARAY • *THE INTOUCHABLES*   *Page 162*
74 LA MAISON DE SERGE GAINSBOURG • *GAINSBOURG: A HEROIC LIFE*   *Page 166*
75 ÉCOLE NATIONALE SUPÉRIEURE DES BEAUX-ARTS • *GAINSBOURG: A HEROIC LIFE*   *Page 167*
76 DEYROLLE • *MIDNIGHT IN PARIS*   *Page 168*
77 LES DEUX MAGOTS • *THE INTOUCHABLES*   *Page 172*
78 LE CAFÉ DE FLORE • *LOVE LASTS THREE YEARS*   *Page 174*
79 LIPP • *TANGUY*   *Page 176*
80 LE CAFÉ DE LA MAIRIE • *THE DISCREET*   *Page 178*
81 L'ÉGLISE SAINT-SULPICE • *THE DA VINCI CODE*   *Page 179*

QUARTIER LATIN
Page 180

82 LA BUVETTE DES MARIONNETTES • *THE INTOUCHABLES*   *Page 182*
83 POLIDOR • *MIDNIGHT IN PARIS*   *Page 184*
84 ESPACE ACCATTONE • *2 DAYS IN PARIS*   *Page 187*
85 DUBOIS • *CONVERSATIONS WITH MY GARDENER*   *Page 188*
86 LE MARCHÉ MAUBERT • *CHANGE OF PLANS*   *Page 190*
87 SAINT-ÉTIENNE-DU-MONT • *MIDNIGHT IN PARIS*   *Page 191*
88 LA BIBLIOTHÈQUE SAINTE-GENEVIÈVE • *HUGO*   *Page 192*
89 THE BOMBARDIER • *'LOLITA' – THE PLAYERS*   *Page 194*
90 LE PIANO VACHE • *GOOD OLD DAZE*   *Page 197*
91 LA PISCINE MUNICIPALE PONTOISE • *THREE COLOURS: BLUE*   *Page 200*
92 SHAKESPEARE AND COMPANY • *BEFORE SUNSET*   *Page 202*
93 LE CAVEAU DE LA HUCHETTE • *HAPPINESS NEVER COMES ALONE*   *Page 204*
94 LAPÉROUSE • *GAINSBOURG: A HEROIC LIFE*   *Page 206*

PORT-ROYAL/JARDIN DES PLANTES
Page 208

95   LA COUPOLE • *HUNTING AND GATHERING*   *Page 210*
96   LA CLOSERIE DES LILAS • *SAGAN*   *Page 212*
97   LE VERRE À PIED • *AMÉLIE*   *Page 214*
98   LE STUDIO DES URSULINES • *JULES AND JIM*   *Page 216*
99   LES GRANDES SERRES DU JARDIN DES PLANTES • *A MONSTER IN PARIS*   *Page 217*
100 LES CAILLOUX • *DELICACY*   *Page 218*
101 LA CAVE LA BOURGOGNE • *MUNICH*   *Page 220*

01	L'HÔTEL DE SOUBISE	CULTURE	MARIE-ANTOINETTE
02	L'HÔTEL DE ROHAN	CULTURE	'QUARTIER DES ENFANTS ROUGES' – PARIS, I LOVE YO
03	LE GEORGES	RESTAURANT	THE STORY OF MY LIFE
04	L'ÉTOILE MANQUANTE	BAR	A HAPPY EVENT
05	L'ANNEXE	BISTRO	POLISSE
06	PAUL	BISTRO	MIDNIGHT IN PARIS
07	KONG	RESTAURANT	TELL NO ONE

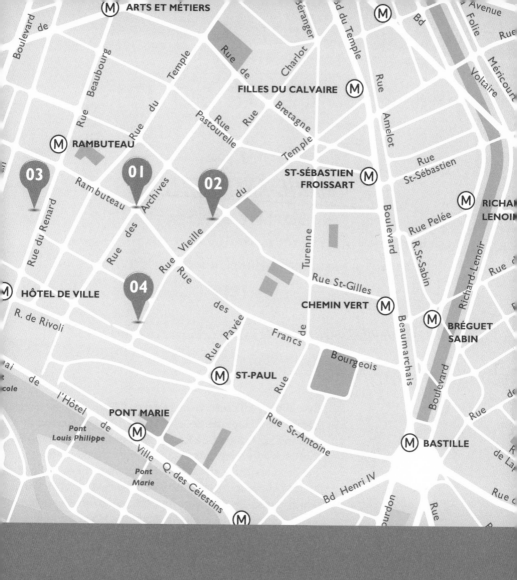

ARTS ET MÉTIERS

FILLES DU CALVAIRE

RAMBUTEAU

03

01

02

ST-SÉBASTIEN
FROISSART

RICHARD
LENOIR

04

HÔTEL DE VILLE

R. de Rivoli

Rue St-Gilles

CHEMIN VERT

BRÉGUET
SABIN

Rue Pavée

Francs

Bourgeois

ST-PAUL

PONT MARIE

Pont
Louis Philippe

Rue St-Antoine

BASTILLE

Pont
Marie

Q. des Célestins

Bd Henri IV

HÔTEL DE VILLE
MARAIS

L'HÔTEL DE SOUBISE

location for:

MARIE-ANTOINETTE

by SOFIA COPPOLA

with KIRSTEN DUNST, JASON SCHWARTZMAN, RIP TORN, MOLLY SHANNON,

ASIA ARGENTO, MARIANNE FAITHFULL, JUDY DAVIS, STEVE COOGAN

• 2006 •

Marie-Antoinette discovers the Château de Versailles

L'HÔTEL DE SOUBISE
-
60, rue des Francs-Bourgeois
75003 Paris
-
Ⓜ Rambuteau
-
☎ 01 40 27 60 96
www.archivesnationales.
culture.gouv.fr/anparis

Price:
★★☆☆☆

WATCH THE TRAILER

See also:
la Galerie dorée
de la Banque de France

Built in the 14th century, the Hotel de Clisson, then de Guise, became the Hotel de Soubise in the 18th century when it was sold to François de Rohan, who completely redesigned it to look as it does today. Although its walls bore witness to the decision of the terrible St Bartholomew's Eve, the place is also famous for having hosted resplendent royal parties at which works by Corneille and Marc-Antoine Charpentier were performed. Like the neighbouring Hotel de Rohan, it was acquired by the State in 1808 and chosen by Napoleon III to become, in 1867, the Museum of French History. Today the Hotel de Soubise also houses the headquarters of the National Archives, which preserve the Declaration of the Rights of Man and of the Citizen of 1789. In addition to exhibitions, conferences and visits, the public can enjoy music at this prestigious venue at the 'Jeunes Talents' (young talent) concerts, which continue the historical musical tradition of the 'Concerts des amateurs' of the 18th century.

The princess's drawing room of the Hotel de Soubise, which is decorated with wood panelling and embellished with pastel blue paintings, was used as the setting for a scene to simulate Versailles.

L'HÔTEL DE ROHAN

location for:

'QUARTIER DES ENFANTS ROUGES' – PARIS, I LOVE YOU

by OLIVIER ASSAYAS

with MAGGIE GYLLENHAAL, JOANA PREISS, LIONEL DRAY, NICOLAS MAURY

• 2006 •

Maggie Gyllenhaal awaits her scene

L'HÔTEL DE ROHAN

-

87, rue Vieille-du-Temple
75003 Paris

-

Ⓜ Rambuteau

-

☎ 01 40 27 60 96
www.archivesnationales.
culture.gouv.fr/anparis/

Price:
★★☆☆☆

WATCH THE TRAILER

This mansion was built in 1705 by the architect Pierre-Alexis Delamair for the Rohan family after their purchase of the neighbouring Hotel de Soubise, whose grounds it shares. Built for their son, the Bishop of Strasbourg, before he was appointed Cardinal of Rohan, the mansion was home to four cardinals, including Louis-René-Edouard de Rohan, who was involved in the famous Affair of the Diamond Necklace. Napoleon I made it the headquarters of the imperial printing works while choosing the Hotel de Soubise to house the National Archives. While the latter building remains its headquarters, the Hotel de Rohan today looks after a part of the National Archives, in particular the archives of all Parisian notaries and of major historic exhibitions. Its majestic Classical façade with its pilasters and columns, its former stables and its 'cabinet aux singes' (monkey cabinet), decorated with exotic travel scenes, recalls the site's rich history.

The Hotel de Rohan provided the perfect backdrop for staging Maggie Gyllenhaal and her sumptuous white wedding dress in a period film.

LE GEORGES

location for:

THE STORY OF MY LIFE

by LAURENT TIRARD

with ÉDOUARD BAER, MARIE-JOSÉE CROZE, CLOVIS CORNILLAC,

ALICE TAGLIONI, ÉRIC BERGER

• 2004 •

Édouard Baer eavesdrops on a conversation at the next table

LE GEORGES
-
Centre national d'art et de
culture Georges Pompidou
19, rue Beaubourg
75004 Paris
-
Ⓜ Rambuteau
-
☎ 01 44 78 47 99
maisonthierrycostes.com

Price:
★★★★☆

WATCH THE TRAILER

High up on the sixth (top) floor of the Pompidou Centre, Le Georges looks proudly down over the rooftops, offering one of the most spectacular views in Paris. One of the Costes restaurants, Le Georges was designed in 2000 by Dominique Jakob and Brendan McFarlane with an ultracontemporary interior that is true to the spirit of the centre, which is entirely devoted to the modern art it houses. In these state-of-the-art, futuristic surroundings, guests can enjoy innovative new-wave world cuisine or rediscover classic dishes. Hidden away in an alcove, the Pink Bar welcomes vodka fans with some explosive cocktails. Finally, the restaurant's large terrace – its crown jewel – provides a breath of cool, chic air and is very popular on sunny days.

The immaculate setting of Le Georges, a restaurant famous for its elite business lunches, perfectly suited the director as the location for the interview conducted by Edouard Baer as a charming journalist in the film's opening scene.

L'ÉTOILE MANQUANTE

location for:

A HAPPY EVENT

by RÉMI BEZANÇON

with LOUISE BOURGOIN, PIO MARMAI, JOSIANE BALASKO,

GABRIELLE LAZURE, THIERRY FRÉMONT

• 2011 •

A final face-to-face between Louise Bourgoin and Pio Marmai

L'ÉTOILE
MANQUANTE
-
34, rue Vieille-du-Temple
75004 Paris
-
Ⓜ Saint-Paul
-
☎ 01 42 72 48 34
www.cafeine.com

Price:
★☆☆☆☆

WATCH THE TRAILER

L'Étoile Manquante is a galaxy of calm in the busy Marais district. The attractiveness of its decor, part starry vault, part old-fashioned bistro, gathers a clientele of locals and tourists who come to enjoy a drink or a bite away from the hustle and bustle of the streets. Its lovely little terrace also makes it a popular place for summertime aperitifs under the stars. An amusing technical detail: there is a little train that runs between the girls' and boys' toilets.

L'ANNEXE

location for:

POLISSE

by MAÏWENN

with KARIN VIARD, JOEYSTARR, MARINA FOÏS, NICOLAS DUVAUCHELLE,

KAROLE ROCHER, EMMANUELLE BERCOT

• 2011 •

Marina Foïs supports Karin Viard on the day of her divorce

Brought into the film for its proximity to the Palais de Justice (law courts), throughout the day this Parisian bistro welcomes a mix of magistrates, regulars and tourists seduced by a quirky menu written in legal jargon: from the *paniers à salade* (Black Marias) and the mise en accusation (indictment) of the pork platter, to the *Mesrine* (an infamous French criminal) omelette and the *garde à vue* (custody) of sausage and chips, all the brasserie's dishes appear without summons in judiciary style.

L'ANNEXE
-
5, bd. du Palais
75004 Paris
-
Ⓜ Cité
-
Price:
★☆☆☆☆

WATCH THE TRAILER

PAUL

location for:

MIDNIGHT IN PARIS

by WOODY ALLEN

with OWEN WILSON, RACHEL MCADAMS, MICHAEL SHEEN,

MARION COTILLARD, KATHY BATES, CARLA BRUNI-SARKOZY

• 2011 •

Owen Wilson loses his mind over Marion Cotillard

PAUL
-
15, place Dauphine
75001 Paris
-
Ⓜ Pont-Neuf
-
☎ 01 43 54 21 48

Price:
★★★☆☆

WATCH THE TRAILER

See also:
Le Bristol, Musée Rodin,
Deyrolle, Polidor,
Saint-Étienne-du-Mont,
Shakespeare and Company

In the heart of historic Paris on the Ile de la Cité, Paul has the perfect location on the beautiful Place Dauphine, where memories of Simone Signoret and Yves Montand linger on. Behind its low door, the delightfully old-fashioned Parisian bistro welcomes guests into impeccable surroundings: immaculate tablecloths, elegant vermillion-red banquettes, slightly faded murals, dark wood panelling, all supported by service of the highest quality. Frequented mostly by men from the Quai des Orfèvres at lunchtime, the restaurant also lends itself to romantic dinners come nightfall. You may even bump into celebrities who have come to dine incognito in this charming hideaway. The menu offers high-quality French cuisine – *œufs mayonnaise*, *andouillette*, or even *blanquette de veau à l'ancienne* – simple dishes steeped in tradition, served in quiet, comfortable surroundings.

Against the backdrop of the restaurant's Parisian retro decor, Woody Allen was able to shoot one of the most romantic night-time scenes of his film. The bistro also hosted the TV mini-series The *Blue Bicycle* with the divine Lætitia Casta.

KONG

location for:

TELL NO ONE

by GUILLAUME CANET

with FRANÇOIS CLUZET, MARIE-JOSÉE CROZE, ANDRÉ DUSSOLLIER,

KRISTIN SCOTT THOMAS, JEAN ROCHEFORT

• 2006 •

Kristin Scott Thomas offers indispensable support to François Cluzet

....

KONG
-
1, rue du Pont-Neuf
75001 Paris
-
Ⓜ Pont-Neuf
-
☎ 01 40 39 09 00
www.kong.fr
-
Price:
★★★☆☆

WATCH THE TRAILER

See also:
le Grand Colbert

In asking Philippe Starck to create a restaurant that would immortalise Paris while at the same time immersing itself in Japanese culture, Laurent Taieb presented the two top floors of the Kenzo flagship with an astonishing gift. The cuisine is accomplished by the dynamic duo of Fumiko Kono, a Tokyoite who has been in love with Paris for more than ten years, and Richard Pommiès, a chef from Perpignan. Dishes exhibit traditional flavours reinvented with a Japanese twist and are served in surroundings that could be from an unlikely 18th century manga. Whether you choose to dine under the stunning panoramic glass roof facing the beautiful Pont-Neuf, have a drink on the Gallery terrace or relax on the first level while listening to a playlist selected by Béatrice Ardisson, Kong offers a unique, all-inclusive experience and an extravagant world that will tempt you back again.

Guillaume Canet, a childhood friend of Laurent Taieb's, had the privilege of filming at Kong. The restaurant was also seen in *Sex and the City* after the series' producer fell in love with it during an evening spent incognito – an appearance that has made the restaurant famous worldwide.

Photo © Patricia Belair

HÔTEL DE VILLE/MARAIS | 19

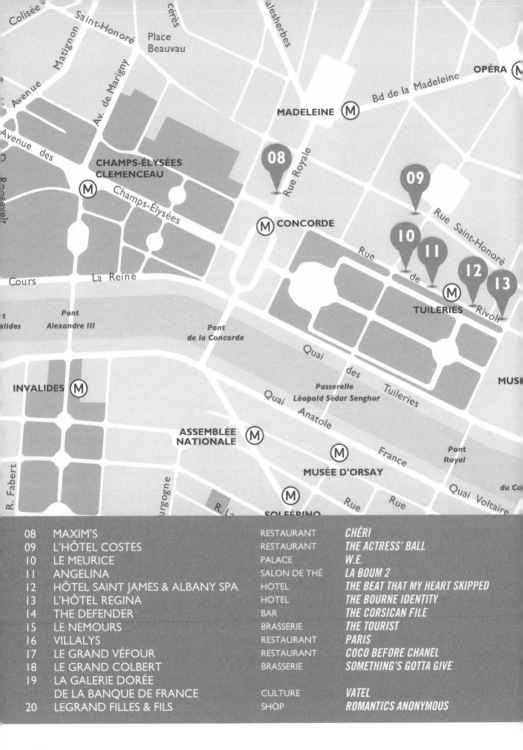

08	MAXIM'S	RESTAURANT	*CHÉRI*
09	L'HÔTEL COSTES	RESTAURANT	*THE ACTRESS' BALL*
10	LE MEURICE	PALACE	*W.E.*
11	ANGELINA	SALON DE THÉ	*LA BOUM 2*
12	HÔTEL SAINT JAMES & ALBANY SPA	HOTEL	*THE BEAT THAT MY HEART SKIPPED*
13	L'HÔTEL REGINA	HOTEL	*THE BOURNE IDENTITY*
14	THE DEFENDER	BAR	*THE CORSICAN FILE*
15	LE NEMOURS	BRASSERIE	*THE TOURIST*
16	VILLALYS	RESTAURANT	*PARIS*
17	LE GRAND VÉFOUR	RESTAURANT	*COCO BEFORE CHANEL*
18	LE GRAND COLBERT	BRASSERIE	*SOMETHING'S GOTTA GIVE*
19	LA GALERIE DORÉE		
	DE LA BANQUE DE FRANCE	CULTURE	*VATEL*
20	LEGRAND FILLES & FILS	SHOP	*ROMANTICS ANONYMOUS*

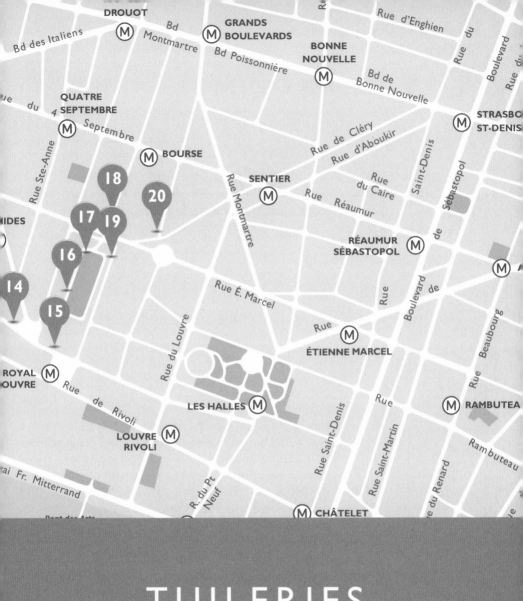

TUILERIES
PALAIS-ROYAL

MAXIM'S

location for:

CHÉRI

by STEPHEN FREARS

with MICHELLE PFEIFFER, RUPERT FRIEND, KATHY BATES

• 2009 •

Chéri returns to his familiar pastimes at Maxim's

MAXIM'S
-
3, rue Royale
75008 Paris
-
Ⓜ Concorde
-
☎ 01 42 65 27 94
www.maxims-de-paris.com
-
Price:
★★★★★

WATCH THE TRAILER

See also:
l'hôtel Regina

Maxim's is more than a restaurant: it is a witness to the history of Parisian nightlife. Opened in 1893, Chez Maxim's, then a small bistro, was soon hosting gilded youth charmed by the English-sounding name of this otherwise very French establishment. Sumptuously redecorated for the World's Fair of 1900 in the Art Nouveau style inspired by fauna, flora and feminine beauty, Maxim's became the place to meet the capital's most famous courtesans, who attracted the elite of the cultural and political worlds. Over the course of the century, the restaurant's opulent setting established it as one of the most prestigious addresses in Paris. When Pierre Cardin bought it in 1981, he transformed the top three floors into a museum, while keeping the main floor open for dinner and themed evenings for well-heeled youth.

Maxim's was repeatedly used as a location by Vincente Minnelli for his legendary *Gigi*, and the restaurant returned to the libertine razzle-dazzle of the Belle Epoque as the centerpiece of Stephen Frears' respectful screen adaptation of Colette's novel.

L'HÔTEL COSTES

location for:

THE ACTRESS' BALL

by MAÏWENN

with MAÏWENN, MÉLANIE DOUTEY, KAROLE ROCHER,

KARIN VIARD, MARINA FOÏS, ROMANE BOHRINGER

• 2009 •

Yvan Attal tries to persuade Mélanie Doutey to join his film

For fifteen years, this luxury hotel near the Place Vendôme has held the prize for the ultimate in glam chic: boycotted by some, adored by others, it is, whatever one might think of it, clearly of the moment, another success orchestrated by Jean-Louis Costes. In an outstanding setting created by interior designer Jacques Garcia, the establishment hosts a cosmopolitan clientele for fashionable stays with an aura of well-being: a swimming pool, spa and hammam are available for guests. Those who just want to enjoy the restaurant can get a taste of the stylish ambiance while sitting out on the subtly charming Italian-style patio on sunny days or at a table in one of the Napoleon III-style lounges. The menu offers a mix of simple but stylish world-fusion dishes and great classics such as steak tartare. Alternatively, you can come sip one of the best mojitos in Paris in the cosy atmosphere of the bar, with subdued lighting and perfumed candles, while listening to the latest in electro-lounge music.

It's hardly surprising that Maïwenn chose the Hotel Costes, the meeting place for the Parisian jet set, for the encounter between the director and the actress in her film.

L'HÔTEL COSTES
-
239, rue Saint-Honoré
75001 Paris

Ⓜ Tuileries
-
☎ 01 42 44 50 00
www.hotelcostes.com
-
Price:
★★★★☆

WATCH THE TRAILER

LE MEURICE

location for:

W.E.

by MADONNA

with ABBIE CORNISH, ANDREA RISEBOROUGH, JAMES D'ARCY,

OSCAR ISAAC, RICHARD COYLE

• 2012 •

*The exiled Edward and Wallis remain banished
from the United Kingdom*

LE MEURICE
-
228, rue de Rivoli
75001 Paris
-
Ⓜ Tuileries
-
☎ 01 44 58 10 10
www.meuricehotel.fr
-
Price:
★★★★★

WATCH THE TRAILER

Built in 1835, Le Meurice is today one of Paris' few remaining palaces. Although it is has the perfect location opposite the Jardin des Tuileries between the Place de la Concorde and the Musée du Louvre, it is its unparalleled elegance – a perfectly harmonious mix of 21st-century luxury, 18th-century refinement and the timeless French art of hospitality – that has won it its prestige. Subtly redecorated by Starck in 2007, the hotel has lost nothing of the unique avant-garde touch that has distinguished it since its opening, when it hosted English tourists arriving in Paris or later, when it welcomed Salvador Dalí and his escapades for at least a month every year for thirty years in what is now Suite 102. Because it received world leaders such as Franklin D. Roosevelt, the Prince of Wales and the Shah of Persia, it has also been nicknamed the 'hotel of kings'.

The sequences showing public areas such as the revolving door and the lobby were shot at Le Meurice. But the suite, the scene of Wallis Simpson and Edward VIII's love affair in exile, was entirely recreated and decorated as an identical copy on set by Madonna's film crew.

ANGELINA

location for:

LA BOUM 2

by CLAUDE PINOTEAU

with SOPHIE MARCEAU, BRIGITTE FOSSEY, CLAUDE BRASSEUR, DENISE GREY

• 1982 •

Vic and Poupette take stock of their love lives over tea

ANGELINA
-
226, rue de Rivoli
75001 Paris
-
Ⓜ Tuileries
-
☎ 01 42 60 82 00
www.angelina-paris.fr
-
Price:
★★☆☆☆

Claude Pinoteau chose Angelina and its timeless style as the setting for Denise Grey to tell the eventful secrets of her love life to Sophie Marceau, who, with all the wisdom of her sixteen years, is very forthcoming with advice.

Founded in 1903 by Antoine Rumpelmayer, an Austrian confectioner, who named it after his daughter-in-law, the Angelina salon de thé flourished over the course of the century, delivering high-quality sweets and sophisticated luxury in the finest French gastronomic tradition. Frequented since its opening by the cultural elite, including Coco Chanel and Marcel Proust, its interior design by Édouard-Jean Niermans takes us back to the ambience of the Belle Epoque of the salon's early years, with its splendid gilding, elegant marble pedestal tables, fine tableware and smartly dressed waiters and waitresses. The young pastry chef, Sébastien Bauer, trained under Pierre Hermé and continues to drive customers wild with the salon's unmissable classic: the 'Mont-Blanc', an incredible meringue served with vanilla-flavored whipped cream and covered with chestnut cream 'spaghetti'. Six hundred of them are served daily in the salon or in the shop to be taken to-go.

HÔTEL SAINT JAMES & ALBANY SPA

location for:

THE BEAT THAT MY HEART SKIPPED

by JACQUES AUDIARD

with ROMAIN DURIS, NIELS ARESTRUP, EMMANUELLE DEVOS,

JONATHAN ZACCAÏ, AURE ATIKA

• 2005 •

Romain Duris provokes the Russians

HÔTEL
SAINT JAMES
& ALBANY SPA

-

202, rue de Rivoli
75001 Paris

-

Ⓜ Tuileries

-

☎ 01 44 58 43 21
www.saintjamesalbany.com

Price:
★★★★☆

WATCH THE TRAILER

Beneath the arcades of the Rue de Rivoli and opposite the Jardin des Tuileries, l'hôtel Saint James & Albany Spa has an exceptional location just a stone's throw from the Musée du Louvre and the Place Vendôme. In a 17th century building, 200 luxury rooms and suites decorated in ochre and fruity tones and furnished in Louis Philippe style, are arranged around a courtyard in which guests are welcomed in a sophisticated ambiance. But the hotel's supreme asset lies in its wellness centre, which comprises an 'After the Rain' spa, a fitness centre and, above all, a superb 15 x 4 m ozone-treated soft-water swimming pool, where swimmers can relax under the soft blue light reflecting off the stone walls. The 202 restaurant serves creative cuisine in the garden while the Saint James bar's intimate and stylish atmosphere is perfect for convivial moments. Business meetings are also hosted, in areas that are equipped for holding seminars and for other professional needs.

In the hotel's pool area, the director was able to reproduce the original decor of the swimming pool in *Fingers* for his remake.

An exception location within a stone's throw of the Musée du Louvre and the Place Vendôme

L'HÔTEL REGINA

location for:

THE BOURNE IDENTITY

by DOUG LIMAN

with MATT DAMON, CHRIS COOPER, CLIVE OWEN, FRANKA POTENTE

• 2002 •

Matt Damon sends Franka Potente to get Mr. Kane's bill

Opened for the World's Fair of 1900, this luxury hotel was founded by Léonard Tauber, a great art lover, who assembled the most talented artists and cabinetmakers of the time to aggrandize his work. His granddaughter, Françoise Baverez, carries on the long family tradition, selecting with the same high standards the best craftsmen and women for its regular renovations.

The hotel has an exceptional location at the very heart of Paris, right in the middle of historical and cultural sites and near the main shopping streets. The comfortable rooms and luxury suites have an unobstructed view of the Eiffel Tower and the Jardin des Tuileries. Other stylish features of the Regina are its lovely shaded courtyard, the perfect peaceful haven in which to take afternoon tea with Ladurée pâtisseries or lunch à la plancha, and its cosy English bar with original creations such as the 'Mojit'eau' alcohol-free cocktail.

This majestic Art Nouveau interior, symbolising luxury *à la française*, has charmed many directors: Stephan Frears for *Chéri* and Luc Besson for *Nikita*, as well as Doug Liman for *The Bourne Identity*.

L'HÔTEL REGINA
-
2, place des Pyramides
75001 Paris
-
Ⓜ Tuileries
-
☎ 01 42 60 31 10
www.regina-hotel.com
-
Price:
★★★★☆

WATCH THE TRAILER

THE DEFENDER

location for:

THE CORSICAN FILE

by ALAIN BERBÉRIAN

with CHRISTIAN CLAVIER, JEAN RENO, CATERINA MURINO, DIDIER FLAMAND

• 2004 •

Christian Clavier brings the Yellow Dragon mission to an end

THE DEFENDER
-
Hôtel du Louvre
1, place André-Malraux
75001 Paris
-
Ⓜ Palais-Royal or
Musée-du-Louvre
-
☎ 01 44 58 37 89
www.hoteldulouvre.com
-
Price:
★★☆☆☆

WATCH THE TRAILER

This hotel bar provides the perfect setting for the beginning of the film where Christian Clavier is spying on a wealthy businessman.

The Defender, from the name of a great scotch whisky made by Taittinger, lies at the heart of the Hotel du Louvre. This intimate bar, designed in a Napoleon III style, has an intimate atmosphere and sumptuous gold, red and black decor. A dynamic team, with impeccable service, carefully prepare inventive house cocktails while whisky lovers are spoilt for choice with a selection of whiskies ranging between ten and 30 years old. Finally, there is a choice of alcoholic beverages from around the world, allowing melancholic international guests to recharge their batteries. Grilled steaks and tartare headline on the menu to satisfy the heartiest appetites, while for those prefer just a snack, there is a selection of Iberian hams and various canapés, including foie gras on spice-bread. You will find an eclectic clientele here: businessmen during the week, tourists at weekends and discriminating Parisians on Thursday and Friday evenings looking for an intimate night out when there are jazz concerts here.

LE NEMOURS

location for:

THE TOURIST

by FLORIAN HENCKEL VON DONNERSMARCK

with ANGELINA JOLIE, JOHNNY DEPP, TIMOTHY DALTON, BRUNO WOLKOWITCH

• 2010 •

Angelina Jolie receives a registered letter from Alexander Pearce

LE NEMOURS
-
2, place Colette
75001 Paris
-
Ⓜ Palais-Royal or
Musée-du-Louvre
-
☎ 01 42 61 34 14
-
Price:
★★☆☆☆

WATCH THE TRAILER

On the beautiful Place Colette, the delightfully quaint Le Nemours serves unpretentious brasserie dishes: croque-monsieur, steak and chips, and 'Molière' and 'Comédienne' salads in homage to the Comédie Française, which is next door to the restaurant. In fact, it's not uncommon, in the evening, to see actors who've come to celebrate their performance in the brasserie's welcoming ambiance. During the day, its clientele is made up of businessmen meeting up for a working drink amidst tourists who, exhausted by the Musée du Louvre, are treating themselves to an ice cream on one of the capital's most beautiful terraces.

This huge space was a major asset for the film's producers because it enabled them to deploy all the equipment and the 200-strong film crew and 70 extras needed for the shoot. The presence of Angelina Jolie created hysteria from 8.30am and the excitement reached its climax when Brad Pitt joined her on set. Le Nemours has often been chosen by the film industry: Jean Becker filmed Jean-Pierre Darroussin and Daniel Auteuil on its terrace in Conversations with My Gardener and François Cluzet missed a tryst here in The Intouchables.

VILLALYS

location for:

PARIS

by CÉDRIC KLAPISCH

with ROMAIN DURIS, JULIETTE BINOCHE, MÉLANIE LAURENT,

FABRICE LUCHINI, KARIN VIARD

• 2008 •

Fabrice Luchini hesitates to put his scholarship to use in television

VILLALYS
-
30, rue Montpensier
75001 Paris
-
Ⓜ Palais-Royal or
Musée-du-Louvre
-
☎ 01 42 61 85 99
-
Price:
★★☆☆☆

WATCH THE TRAILER

See also:
Aux Folies

Do you want to have lunch in the tranquility of one of the most beautiful gardens in Paris? The terrace at Villalys awaits you from March onwards. Making the most of the splendid setting of the Palais-Royal gardens, it opens out onto the only one in the capital to have received the endorsement 'Remarquable'. The delightful paths lined with red chestnut trees and lime trees pruned into canopies, lawns bordered with flowerbeds, and the central fountain provide a peace that will be disturbed only by the clinking of cutlery or a game of pétanque, unless you talk, between mouthfuls, about the temporary sculpture exhibition on view. In less clement weather, the interior of the restaurant designed by Olivier Gossart welcomes you into chic, understated surroundings that are in perfect keeping with the nearby regal elegance. The menu offers inventive cuisine with a particular penchant for North African specialities such as couscous and tajines.

At the very hub of France's rich history, the Villalys could not be bettered as a setting for Fabrice Luchini playing a renowned Parisian historian.

LE GRAND VÉFOUR

location for:

COCO BEFORE CHANEL

by ANNE FONTAINE

with AUDREY TAUTOU, BENOÎT POELVOORDE, MARIE GILLAIN,

ALESSANDRO NIVOLA, EMMANUELLE DEVOS

• 2009 •

Benoît Poelvoorde gets to know the real Coco

LE GRAND VÉFOUR
-
17, rue du Beaujolais
75001 Paris
-
Ⓜ Palais-Royal or
Musée-du-Louvre or Bourse
-
☎ 01 42 96 56 27
www.grand-vefour.com
-
Price:
★★★★★

WATCH THE TRAILER

In 1784 the chic Café de Chartres opened; in 1820, it became the gourmet restaurant Véfour and was soon frequented by great historical figures, from Bonaparte to Victor Hugo. Louis Vaudale, who already owned the very popular Maxim's, took over the place in 1944 and renamed it the Grand Véfour in tribute to the high-end fine cuisine that would thereafter be served here. The artistic world of Paris flocked to the restaurant and continued to frequent it after the arrival, in 1953, of the chef Raymond Oliver, who continued to uphold its French gastronomic tradition for more than 30 years. In 1991, Guy Martin took over the kitchens before becoming the restaurant's owner 20 years later. His contemporary cuisine, created with seasonal produce, invites you to fabulous flights of flavour at each mouthful. Indeed, you'll embark on an unforgettable journey from the moment the plate is set before you, because this culinary wizard who can pull anything out of his hat also knows how to dress up his dishes, drawing on his other passion: painting. As the restaurant was frequented by Mademoiselle Chanel, it was a logical choice for Anne Fontaine to place her heroine Coco in this splendid location.

LE GRAND COLBERT

location for:

SOMETHING'S GOTTA GIVE

by NANCY MEYERS

with DIANE KEATON, JACK NICHOLSON

• 2004 •

*Jack Nicholson surprises Diane Keaton
in Paris on her birthday*

A Parisian brasserie that has been classified as an historical monument, Le Grand Colbert is named after the minister of Louis XIV. At first a private mansion, then a general store, the building became an inexpensive restaurant in 1900 before its total and elegant restoration in 1985 financed by its owner, the Bibliothèque Nationale (National Library). Behind its splendid façade, a long room with an impressive high ceiling, sculpted pilasters, friezes and bistro banquettes faithfully conveys the inimitable atmosphere of the Paris of a bygone era.

The cuisine is classic: Provençal-style frogs' legs, chilled *foie gras* with Sauternes, fine *sole meunière*, *blanquette de veau* and *crêpes suzette*, the thoroughly traditional dishes being in perfect keeping with this historic establishment.

Nancy Meyers set up the cameras for *Something's Gotta Give* here for more than a week to film nine intense minutes. French films have also made the most of the interior: Jamel Debbouze faces his angel in Luc Besson's *Angel A* and Édouard Baer meets Clovis Cornillac and Alice Taglioni in Lauraent Tirard's *The Story of My Life*.

LE GRAND
COLBERT

-

2, rue Vivienne
75002 Paris

-

Ⓜ Bourse

-

☎ 01 42 86 87 88
www.legrandcolbert.fr

-

Price:
★★★☆☆

WATCH THE TRAILER

LA GALERIE DORÉE DE LA BANQUE DE FRANCE

location for:

VATEL

by ROLAND JOFFÉ

with GÉRARD DEPARDIEU, UMA THURMAN, TIM ROTH

• 2000 •

Tim Roth checks the renovations of the Château de Chantilly before the king's arrival

LA GALERIE DORÉE
-
Banque de France
2, rue de Radziwill
75001 Paris
-
Ⓜ Bourse
-
☎ 01 44 54 19 30

For visiting information:
www.banque-France.fr
-
Price:
★★☆☆☆

WATCH THE TRAILER

In 1635, Louis Phélypeaux de la Vrillère, a wealthy collector, added the finishing touches to his mansion built by François Mansart with a gallery to house his art collection. Ten paintings by Italian masters adorn the walls of the 40-metre long gallery beneath its high ceiling with a fresco by François Perrier. In 1713, it was bought by the Count of Toulouse, who added magnificent Regency-style panelling covered with gold leaf. It thus became the Golden Gallery. This symbol of opulence survived the Revolution by becoming the paper storage depot for the national printing works and the ten paintings were dispersed among museums. In 1811, Napoleon I authorized the Banque de France to move into the building, acquired in 1808. The gallery, which had fallen into disrepair as a result of water infiltrations and soft ground, was entirely demolished and rebuilt in identical fashion in 1865. Since then it has been the jewel of the French financial institution and witness to all the country's major monetary decisions.

Roland Joffé along with Alain Corneau for *All the Mornings of the World* and Sofia Coppola for *Marie-Antoinette* have used the Golden Gallery to return their characters to the Age of Enlightenment.

A great place to visit on European Heritage Days

LEGRAND FILLES & FILS

location for:

ROMANTICS ANONYMOUS

by JEAN-PIERRE AMÉRIS

with ISABELLE CARRÉ, BENOÎT POELVOORDE

• 2010 •

Isabelle Carré presents her new chocolates

LEGRAND
FILLES & FILS
-
1, rue de la Banque
75002 Paris
-
Ⓜ Bourse
-
☎ 01 42 60 07 12
www.caves-legrand.com

Price:
★★☆☆☆

WATCH THE TRAILER

See also:
À la Mère de Famille

This old shop belonging to the Corporation des Epiciers (grocers' corporation) established itself over the years as a great house or tradition, a status that was initiated in 1945 by Pierre Legrand who sold roasted coffee, alcohol and candles. A passion for wine has been handed down for four generations with the aim of unearthing treasure from little-known vineyards for wine-lovers. This expertise has ensured that today Legrand Filles & Fils is ranked as one of Paris's finest wine merchants, where wine tastings and courses take place. A space at the heart of the shop presents a selection of regional charcuteries and cheeses, always matched with a chosen wine. The shop also sells an assortment of biscuits and sweets, including marshmallows and deliciously regressive-tasting toffees to satisfy nostalgic sweet-lovers.

This wine merchant and delicatessen, decorated with old wood panelling behind its original facade, impressed the director, who had been searching for artisans specialized in unearthing old-fashioned treasures in a quaint setting to give the design of his film an authentic feel.

21	LE BRISTOL	PALACE	*MIDNIGHT IN PARIS*
22	LE CLUB 13	RESTAURANT	*L'AVENTURE, C'EST L'AVENTURE*
23	CINÉMA MAC MAHON	CULTURE	*BREATHLESS*
24	TUTTI FIESTA	SHOP	*L'AMOUR C'EST MIEUX À DEUX*
25	LE CENTRE DE TIR DE PARIS		
	DE LA POLICE NATIONALE	EXPERIENCE	*LA FEMME NIKITA*
26	L'HÔTEL RAPHAEL	HOTEL	*HOTEL CHEVALIER*
27	PERSHING HALL	RESTAURANT	*LITTLE WHITE LIES*
28	LE MUSÉE GALLIERA	CULTURE	*THE DEVIL WEARS PRADA*
29	LE TOKYO EAT	RESTAURANT	*HUNTING AND GATHERING*
30	LA MAISON BLANCHE	RESTAURANT	*AVENUE MONTAIGNE*
31	LE PLAZA ATHÉNÉE	PALACE	*AVENUE MONTAIGNE*
32	LES OMBRES	RESTAURANT	*CHANGE OF PLAN*
33	LA TOUR EIFFEL	CULTURE	*A VIEW TO A KILL*
34	MATSURI	RESTAURANT	*THE BIG PICTURE*

ÉTOILE
CHAMPS-ÉLYSÉES

LE BRISTOL

location for:

MIDNIGHT IN PARIS

by WOODY ALLEN

with OWEN WILSON, RACHEL MCADAMS, MICHAEL SHEEN,

MARION COTILLARD, KATHY BATES, CARLA BRUNI-SARKOZY

• 2011 •

Owen Wilson disappears from his hotel room every night

LE BRISTOL
-
112, rue du Fg-Saint-Honoré
75008 Paris
-
Ⓜ Miromesnil
-
☎ 01 53 43 43 00
www.lebristolparis.com
-
Price:
★★★★★
WATCH THE TRAILER

See also:
Paul, Musée Rodin,
Deyrolle, Polidor,
Saint-Étienne-du-Mont,
Shakespeare and Company

Named in honour of the Count of Bristol, who was famous for his love of luxury and comfort, Le Bristol was opened in 1925, in the heart of the Roaring Twenties, in a former private mansion built in 1758 and then transformed into a luxury hotel a stone's throw away from the Palais de l'Élysée. Serving as the home of the American Embassy in 1940, it was the only palace in the capital that escaped requisition. After the Liberation, luxury shops opened in the Saint-Honoré district and the hotel became the favourite haunt of VIPs and international diplomats. Regular renovations have maintained its opulent standards and Le Bristol is also famous for the unparalleled quality of its service, which is much appreciated by numerous film stars, politicians and businessmen. Its panoramic swimming pool overlooking the Paris skyline, its huge French-style garden and its three-starred restaurant, Epicure, add a final touch of perfection.

Woody Allen chose Le Bristol as his Parisian residence during the filming of *Midnight in Paris* and paid tribute to it by having Owen Wilson, his fiancée and her parents stay here in the film.

LE CLUB 13

location for:

L'AVENTURE, C'EST L'AVENTURE

by CLAUDE LELOUCH

with LINO VENTURA, NICOLE COURCEL, ALDO MACCIONE, CHARLES DENNER, JACQUES BREL, CHARLES GÉRARD, YVES ROBERT, JOHNNY HALLYDAY

• 1972 •

Lino Ventura, Jacques Brel and Charles Denner take a lesson in politics

In 1966, following the unexpected accolades bestowed on *A Man and a Woman* – a Palme d'Or at Cannes and an Oscar for Best Screenplay – Claude Lelouch decided to buy premises on Avenue Hoche to create an independent cinema so that he could be self-sufficient, free from having to suffer the setbacks of this often difficult milieu. He called it Club 13, after his favourite number (corresponding to the number of letters in his name), which he'd already used in the name of his production company, Les Films 13. With one of the finest private screening rooms in Paris, accommodating sixty-five large leather armchairs, the venue has notably hosted Charlie Chaplin for a screening of the remastered version of *A King in New York* and Orson Welles for a few days working in Paris in the office. Le Club 13 is also home to a chic restaurant, today decorated with the host's souvenirs, which is open to all for a pleasant lunch. A reception room, often used by film professionals and valued by the media, is available for private hire.

Claude Lelouch used Le Club 13 and its restaurant as a backdrop for Lino Ventura and Jacques Brel in *L'aventure, c'est l'aventure*.

LE CLUB 13
-
15, av. Hoche
75008 Paris
-
Ⓜ Courcelles
-
☎ 01 44 13 11 33
www.lesfilms13.com

Price:
★★★☆☆

WATCH THE TRAILER

CINÉMA MAC MAHON

location for:

BREATHLESS

by JEAN-LUC GODARD

with JEAN-PAUL BELMONDO, JEAN SEBERG,
DANIEL BOULANGER, HENRI-JACQUES HUET

• 1960 •

Jean Seberg takes refuge in the cinema

CINÉMA
MAC MAHON
-
5, av. Mac-Mahon
75017 Paris
-
Ⓜ Charles-de-Gaulle-Étoile
-
☎ 01 43 80 24 81
www.cinemamacmahon.com

Price:
★☆☆☆☆

WATCH THE TRAILER

In its bijou space, this small cinema, with its flamboyant façade and doors, resembles the sort found on Broadway. After you've passed the old-fashioned box office and gone down the steep stairs, the stage curtains, velvet armchairs and red walls set the scene beneath the star-spangled vaults. But before you take up the invitation to relax in comfort, take the time to go run into Jean's ghost in the famous ladies' toilets. Opened in 1938, the Cinéma Mac Mahon is one of the film world's legendary venues in Paris. After the Liberation, it became famous for screening all the American films that had been censored during the occupation. Because of this commitment, it soon afterwards became the haunt of the 'Mac Mahonnians', who swore by four cult film directors: Raoul Walsh, Otto Preminger, Joseph Losey and Fritz Lang. But in the end, the venue will be remembered in the history of cinema for its role in the creating of the *Cahiers du cinema* and the French New Wave. Jean-Luc Godard, assisted by Claude Chabrol, following an idea of François Truffaut's, chose it for *Breathless* for this symbolic reason.

TUTTI FIESTA

location for:

L'AMOUR C'EST MIEUX À DEUX

by ARNAUD LEMORT AND DOMINIQUE FARRUGIA

with VIRGINIE EFIRA, CLOVIS CORNILLAC, MANU PAYET, JONATHAN LAMBERT

• 2010 •

Manu Payet unearths a mariachi hat handmade in Mexico

TUTTI FIESTA
-
47, rue Saint-Ferdinand
75017 Paris
-
Ⓜ Porte-Maillot
-
☎ 01 40 68 77 89
www.tuttifiesta.com
-
Price:
★★☆☆☆

Tutti Fiesta is the Parisian temple devoted to festivities of every kind. Here, just steps from Porte Maillot, in 300 square metres of space, a delightful cornucopia of all the accessories required to organize a successful party or celebration await you: party favours, streamers, paper lanterns, confetti, garlands, balloons, masks and hats. The shop can also help you plan the ultimate birthday tea party or neighbourhood street bash thanks to its complete party decoration kits, invitation cards, extraordinary piñatas, princess or football games for the little ones, as well as a whole heap of tips and tricks for avoiding pre-celebration stress. Finally, of course, a complete range of fancy-dress outfits is available for sale or hire, for cherubs dreaming of being a cowboy or a princess and for older ones wanting to dress up as Marilyn Monroe, a sailor, Red Riding Hood or a sexy maid. Fortunately, the fajita costume with matching green 'guacamole' tights that was offered to Manu Payet doesn't exist, nor does the spinach-free Popeye outfit imagined by Jonathan Lambert, which had the film crew in stitches.

LE CENTRE DE TIR DE PARIS DE LA POLICE NATIONALE

location for:

LA FEMME NIKITA

by LUC BESSON

with ANNE PARILLAUD, TCHÉKY KARYO, JEAN-HUGUES ANGLADE,

JEANNE MOREAU, JEAN RENO, JEAN BOUISE

• 1990 •

Nikita's training

LE CENTRE DE TIR
DE PARIS DE LA
POLICE NATIONALE
-
Parking Étoile-Foch
Level -3
75016 Paris
-
Ⓜ Charles-de-Gaulle-Étoile
-
☎ 01 45 01 81 53
-
Price:
★★★★★
WATCH THE TRAILER

See also:
le Train Bleu

The founder of this police shooting range, Honorary Chief Inspector Raymond Sasia, was General de Gaulle's bodyguard and the first Frenchman to be trained by the FBI, at that time directed by J. Edgar Hoover. On the strength of that experience, he imported the rapid fire method to France. He opened the centre in the early 1960s near the Arc de Triomphe. Today the centre has 1,900 members via sponsorship by an active member, under the strict supervision of instructors of the Police Nationale and the French shooting federation. The irreproachable quality of its facilities has given it an unequivocable reputation: twelve soundproofed and insulated shooting stands with reinforced glazing, equipped with an automatic carrier, a ventilation system against gunpowder odours, and a video screen to gauge performance, allowing members to shoot in complete safety while choosing their target distance.

The reliability of its amenities and the comfort of its clubhouse have provided the ultimate argument for celebrities: Luc Besson filmed *La Femme Nikita* here, Alain Delon trained here for his role in *Pour la peau d'un flic (For a Cop's Hide)* and Yves Montand for his part in *Police Python (The Case Against Ferro)*.

Centre de Tir de Paris
de la Police Nationale

L'HÔTEL RAPHAEL

location for:

HOTEL CHEVALIER

by WES ANDERSON

with NATALIE PORTMAN, JASON SCHWARTZMAN

• 2008 •

*Natalie Portman disturbs
Jason Schwartzman's peaceful retreat*

L'HÔTEL RAPHAEL

-

17, av. Kléber
75116 Paris

-

Ⓜ Kléber

-

☎ 01 53 64 32 00
www.raphael-hotel.com

Price:
★★★★★

The Raphael Hotel is without doubt the most atypical five-star hotel in Paris. This showcase of style was built in 1925 by Léonard Tauber, the founder of the Majestic and the Regina, to offer its VIP clientele a real haven of luxury with an intimate atmosphere. Thanks to its family tradition, this jewel in the crown of the French hotel sector has managed to retain its soul in an unfailingly sumptuous but private milieu. You don't need to spend the night in one of its eighty-three rooms to enjoy, in the fabulous wood-panelled English bar, a cocktail in hommage to Gainsbourg, who chose this as his second home. And if you're not sufficiently struck by the new restaurant and its new chef Amandine Chaignot, or overwhelmed by the gallery, go up to the Raphael's seventh-floor terrace with its teak furniture surrounded by fruit trees for a 360-degree view of Paris.

This unique atmosphere has inspired many directors, including Wes Anderson, who sublimely filmed a naked Natalie Portman in this boutique hotel, and Nicole Garcia for *Place Vendôme*.

Robert de Niro is said to have named his son Raphael after his numerous stays in this hotel

PERSHING HALL

location for:

LITTLE WHITE LIES

by GUILLAUME CANET

with GILLES LELLOUCHE, MARION COTILLARD, FRANÇOIS CLUZET, BENOÎT MAGIMEL,

VALÉRIE BONNETON, PASCALE ARBILLOT, LAURENT LAFITTE, JEAN DUJARDIN

• 2010 •

Benoît Magimel reveals his feelings to François Cluzet

PERSHING HALL
-
49, rue Pierre-Charon
75008 Paris
-
Ⓜ George V
-
☎ 01 58 36 58 36
www.pershinghall.com

Price:
★★★★☆

WATCH THE TRAILER

See also:
le Mécano Bar

Pershing Hall is named after the American general John Pershing, who lived here when it was a private mansion during the First World War. The building, which is owned by the United States government, has been rented since 1998 to house a fashionable restaurant. Designed by the architect Andrée Putnam, the restaurant is on two levels: an ultra-chic patio, open to the sky with a sliding glass roof, and a terrace level. One wall of the court has been transformed into a vertical garden by Patrick Blanc and contains more than 300 tree varieties and plants from around the world. The establishment provides a continuous service, from breakfast for the area's yuppies to elegant dining, for which it offers the perfect romantic setting for a first date. On Sundays, a copious brunch is served on the patio to those in the know. The menu is a subtle mix of traditional French with fine cuts of meat and refined world fusion cuisine, like caramelised Black Cod with a wakame salad.

Guillaume Canet came here many times as a client to check the place out before choosing it for his film.

LE MUSÉE GALLIERA

location for:

THE DEVIL WEARS PRADA

by DAVID FRANKEL

with MERYL STREEP, ANNE HATHAWAY, EMILY BLUNT, STANLEY TUCCI

• 2006 •

Meryl Streep surprises everyone at the celebration for James Holt

LE MUSÉE GALLIERA

-
10, av. Pierre-Ier-de-Serbie
75116 Paris
-
Ⓜ léna
-
☎ 01 56 52 86 00
www.galliera.paris.fr

Price:
★☆☆☆☆

WATCH THE TRAILER

Named after the Genoese duchess who had it built in the nineteenth century, the Galliera Palace reemerged in 1977 as the museum of fashion of the City of Paris, having previously been the museum of industrial art then let as a high-quality auction house. With its Italian Renaissance-style architecture, imposing courtyard, high painted ceilings and its square, this magnificent building now brings to life three centuries of the history of fashion and costume. Only two sensational temporary exhibitions are offered each year, in order to conserve the textiles that are drawn from a rich source of more than 100,000 articles of clothing and accessories. Thus visitors found themselves dreaming in front of outfits worn by Marlene Dietrich in the cinema or trotting around in the dance-hall and dressing room recreated for the 'Années folles' (Roaring Twenties) exhibition. The museum also has a resource centre that contains exhibition catalogues and fashion magazines.

A perfect veiled reference, the sumptuous interior of the Musée Galliera suited *The Devil Wears Prada* marvelously for Meryl Streep's arrival at the reception in the final scene.

LE TOKYO EAT

location for:

HUNTING AND GATHERING

by CLAUDE BERRI

with AUDREY TAUTOU, GUILLAUME CANET, LAURENT STOCKER, FRANÇOISE BERTIN

• 2007 •

Audrey Tautou and her mother squabble about New Year's Eve

LE TOKYO EAT
-
13, av. du Président-Wilson
75116 Paris
-
Ⓜ Iéna ou Alma-Marceau
-
☎ 01 47 20 00 29
www.palaisdetokyo.com
-
Price:
★★☆☆☆

See also:
la Coupole

After you've paced the corridors of the modern art museum at the Palais de Tokyo, you'll be ready for a break and a bite to eat. The contemporary world of Tokyo Eat revitalizes the concept of museum restaurants with its welcoming atmosphere and its offbeat design: a cathedral-like space with walls and ceilings left deliberately rough, a mixture of colourful chairs and armchairs, round tables, some of them gigantic, orange UFO pendant lights and Roy Lichtenstein-style Pop Art stained glass. The toilets, too, are worth a visit. The large stainless-steel kitchen, which is open onto the restaurant, serves dishes that are a hybrid of local and Asian flavours, an inventive cuisine that will satisfy palates from anywhere in the world. In fine weather, an eclectic clientele of tourists and arty locals invade the huge terrace, which has a view of the Seine and the Eiffel Tower. Booking is highly recommended, as is taking the precaution to come here on foot, or by bike or metro, on Tuesdays and Fridays, when the market makes parking in the vicinity impossible.

In the novel by Anna Gavalda, the original scene wasn't precisely situated, so the director was left free to choose the restaurant.

LA MAISON BLANCHE

location for:

AVENUE MONTAIGNE

by DANIÈLE THOMPSON

with CÉCILE DE FRANCE, ALBERT DUPONTEL, VALÉRIE LEMERCIER,

CLAUDE BRASSEUR, DANI, CHRISTOPHER THOMPSON

• 2006 •

Cécile de France retreats to the roof of the Théâtre des Champs-Elysées

LA MAISON
BLANCHE
-
15, av. Montaigne
75008 Paris
-
Ⓜ Alma-Marceau
-
☎ 01 47 23 55 99
www.maison-blanche.fr

Price:
★★★★☆

WATCH THE TRAILER

See also:
le Plaza Athénée

Opened in 2001, the Maison Blanche has a magnificent view over the very chic Avenue Montaigne from the top of the Art Deco building housing the Théâtre des Champs-Elysées. Singled out as the top restaurant in the world for business lunches in the very serious ranking by *Forbes USA* magazine, the restaurant welcomes its guests in an understated, ultrachic interior designed by Imaad Rahmouni, a disciple of Philippe Starck. You can choose to sit at large, sociable tables, or, for more privacy, in one of the silk-covered alcoves of the 'Baie vitrée' (picture window) dining room with a spectacular view, or at the phosphorescent bar of the 'Mezzanine', which has a terrace for lunch in the open air. In the kitchen, the young chef Sylvain Ruffenart infuses the sensory Languedoc cuisine of the Pourcel brothers with an innovative touch. The colourful dishes are made with fresh, seasonal produce to create a cuisine that is subtle and flavoursome.

In April 2011, an incredible second terrace was opened overlooking Paris and the Eiffel Tower. Danièle Thompson had filmed Cécile de France here on what was then just the roof of the building facing the restaurant.

LE PLAZA ATHÉNÉE

location for:

AVENUE MONTAIGNE

by DANIÈLE THOMPSON

with CÉCILE DE FRANCE, ALBERT DUPONTEL, VALÉRIE LEMERCIER,

CLAUDE BRASSEUR, DANI, CHRISTOPHER THOMPSON

• 2006 •

Albert Dupontel is incensed by the Japanese journalist's questions

The luxurious Plaza Athénée opened in 1911 near the Théâtre des Champs-Élysées. On the strength of this address, it was soon being frequented by the arts world. In 1947, the hotel truly spread its wings thanks to Christian Dior, who chose to open his first shop just a stone's throw away. The Avenue Montaigne subsequently became the hub of haute couture and the Plaza Athénée the in-vogue meeting place for the elite of the fashion and business worlds. A century later, the hotel remains a symbol of opulence à la française thanks to its renovation in 2000, which stylishly combines elegant tradition and trendy innovation. The three-star Alain Ducasse restaurant, Christophe Michalak pâtisseries in La Galerie des Gobelins, the very publicized bar with touchscreen menus and the Dior Institute add their seal of perfection to the sumptuousness of its unique rooms.

Then neighbouring the Montaigne branch of the celebrated Drouot auction house (closed in 2012), the Plaza Athénée was an obvious choice for Danièle Thompson for *Avenue Montaigne*. The hotel was also used as a location for *Proper Attire Required* by Philippe Lioret as well as for the final episodes of the cult series *Sex and the City*.

LE PLAZA ATHÉNÉE
-
25, av. Montaigne
75008 Paris
-
Ⓜ Alma-Marceau
-
☎ 01 53 67 66 65
www.plaza-athenee-paris.fr
Price:
★★★★★

WATCH THE TRAILER

See also:
la Maison blanche

LES OMBRES

location for:

CHANGE OF PLANS

by DANIÈLE THOMPSON

with KARIN VIARD, DANY BOON, MARINA FOÏS, PATRICK BRUEL, EMMANUELLE SEIGNER, CHRISTOPHER THOMPSON, MARINA HANDS, PATRICK CHESNAIS, PIERRE ARDITI

• 2009 •

Christopher Thompson hides his discomfort from an angry Karin Viard

LES OMBRES
-
27, quai Branly
75007 Paris
-
Ⓜ Pont-de-l'Alma
-
☎ 01 47 53 68 00
lesombres-restaurant.com
-
Price:
★★★★☆

WATCH THE TRAILER

See also:
le Zéphyr, la Halle aux Oliviers,
le marché Maubert, le Pure Café,
Point Éphémère

High up on the fifth floor of the Musée du Quai Branly, the gourmet restaurant Les Ombres offers a breathtaking view over the Paris skyline. Jean Nouvel, the museum's architect, was also entirely responsible for the restaurant's interior design, which is dedicated to the Eiffel Tower: everything from furniture to tableware reflects the Iron Lady's play of light and shadow. At lunchtime, business customers crowd here to enjoy the modern dishes created by chef Jean-François Ozon, whose cuisine, a subtle mix of finesse and flavour, is, like the museum, open to the world. The desserts are made by Pascal Chanceau, formerly of Drouant. In the afternoon, the continuous service enables clients to avail themselves of one of the most beautiful terraces in Paris for a light break and enjoy something sweet with a Mariages Frères tea or infusions from the herbalists of the Palais-Royal. In the evening, the glass roof provides a romantic setting for couples to dine under the stars, opposite the sparkling Eiffel Tower.

Danièle Thompson had the unique privilege of being able to film in this location and thus bring together Karin Viard and her co-star Christopher Thompson over a business lunch.

LA TOUR EIFFEL

location for:

A VIEW TO A KILL

by JOHN GLEN

with ROGER MOORE, CHRISTOPHER WALKEN,

TANYA ROBERTS, GRACE JONES, PATRICK MCNEE

• 1985 •

Roger Moore chases Grace Jones to the top

LA TOUR EIFFEL
-
Av. Gustave-Eiffel
75007 Paris
-
Ⓜ Bir-Hakeim
-
☎ 0892 70 12 39
www.tour-eiffel.fr
-
Price:
★★☆☆☆

WATCH THE TRAILER

The Eiffel Tower is cinema's most beautiful and faithful Parisian fiancée, whose elegant looks have been cast in lavish cameos more often than any other profile in Paris. We did think about relating here the tower's history, its levels, lifts, Michelin-starred Jules Verne restaurant and the seven million people from across the globe who visit it every year, making it one of the most visited monuments in the world, but we chose instead to remember the unforgettable fantasies that it has inspired in filmmakers and that have contributed to the unwavering affection we feel for it. It was lit up by a snap of heartthrob Hippolyte Girardot's fingers in *Love Without Pity*, subjected to violence in *Mars Attacks*, *Independence Day*, *Armageddon* and *War of the Worlds*, and continually referenced in François Truffaut's films, but it's undoubtedly the chase scene on its staircases in *A View to a Kill*, with Roger Moore and Grace Jones racing up to the summit for the legendary parachute jump, that provides the most exhilarating tribute to our beloved Eiffel Tower.

MATSURI

location for:

THE BIG PICTURE

by ÉRIC LARTIGAU

with ROMAIN DURIS, CATHERINE DENEUVE, MARINA FOÏS, NIELS ARESTRUP

• 2010 •

Catherine Deneuve puts Romain Duris in shock

MATSURI
-
2-4, rue de Passy
75016 Paris
-
Ⓜ Passy
-
☎ 01 42 24 96 85
www.matsuri.fr
-
Price:
★★☆☆☆

WATCH THE TRAILER

Matsuri takes its name from the popular festivals of the Land of the Rising Sun, in which the Japanese celebrate local folklore and friends gather together to feast on specialities. In chic, sleek Japanese surroundings, plates pass by on a conveyor belt, enticing hands to reach out and grab them. Alongside heavenly sushi and sashimi, yakitori and maki, are Japanese desserts such as *daifuku*, rice cakes stuffed with sweetened red bean paste, and *gyunyukan*, coconut jelly with dried fruit. The restaurant also serves ephemeral creations such as green tea crème brulée. Matsuri is also eco-friendly: it banned Mediterranean bluefin tuna, threatened by overfishing, from its menu several years ago, replacing it with responsibly fished yellowfin tuna, and the rice is now all certified organic. A reliable setting for the long dramatic sequence adapted for film from the novel by Douglas Kennedy, Matsuri can also be seen in *LOL* for a face-to-face encounter between Sophie Marceau and Alexandre Astier, then separated.

35	L'AUBERGE PYRÉNÉES CÉVENNES	RESTAURANT	*OSS 117: CAIRO, NEST OF SPIES*
36	L'HÔTEL DU NORD	RESTAURANT	*HOTEL DU NORD*
37	L'ATMOSPHÈRE	BISTRO	*RUSSIAN DOLLS*
38	POINT ÉPHÉMÈRE	CULTURE	*'LOLITA' – THE PLAYERS*
39	L'HÔTEL KUNTZ	HOTEL	*BELOVED*
40	LE BRADY	CULTURE	*LOVE SONGS*
41	LE PASSAGE BRADY	EXPERIENCE	*FRANTIC*
42	JULIEN	BRASSERIE	*LA VIE EN ROSE*

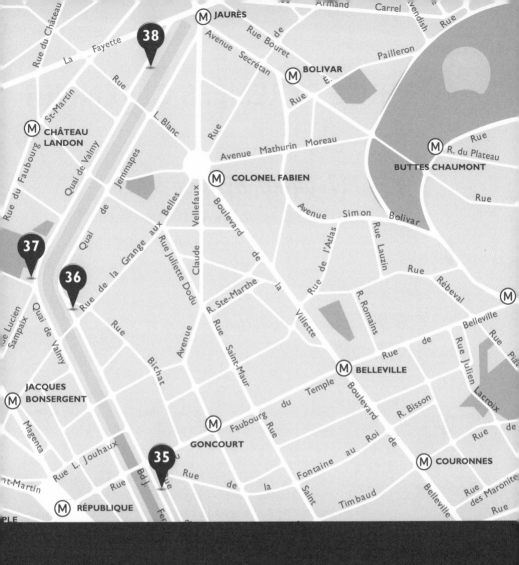

SAINT-DENIS
SAINT-MARTIN

L' AUBERGE PYRÉNÉES CÉVENNES

location for:

OSS 117: CAIRO, NEST OF SPIES

by MICHEL HAZANAVICIUS

with JEAN DUJARDIN, BÉRÉNICE BEJO, AURE ATIKA

• 2006 •

OSS 117 has come to be briefed for his next mission

L'AUBERGE
PYRÉNÉES CÉVENNES

-

106, rue de la Folie-Méricourt
75011 Paris

-

Ⓜ République
or Goncourt

-

☎ 01 43 57 33 78

-

Price:
★★★☆☆

WATCH THE TRAILER

Don't be put off by the drawn white curtains: this former biscuit factory, now an authentic inn, is open. As soon as you cross the threshold, you'll receive a warm, provincial-style welcome. Brimming with humour and conviviality, Françoise Constentin, owner since 1998, knows how to receive guests: checked tablecloths, cloth napkins, hams hanging from wooden beams on the ceiling and a trophy boar's head on the wall.

And if you throw out the famous line from the film "Comment est votre blanquette ?" ("How's your stew?"), you'll immediately establish a friendly rapport. Daniel, Françoise's husband, is in charge in the kitchen, where he concocts hearty and tasty dishes for a menu that contains a mixture of Lyonnaise specialities and delights from southwest France. Particularly noteworthy is the divine cassoulet, which takes three days to prepare.

In addition to the politicians who frequent the place, Jean Dujardin is often seen in what is reputedly one of his favourite restaurants. He has been a regular here for years, which was why OSS 117 was filmed here. The late Claude Brosset, who answers the question in this scene, was also a frequent visitor.

The stuffed thrush had a double in OSS 117

L'HÔTEL DU NORD

location for:

HOTEL DU NORD

by MARCEL CARNÉ

with ANNABELLA, ARLETTY, LOUIS JOUVET

• 1938 •

Atmosphere, atmosphere...

It would be impossible not to pay tribute to the legendary Hotel du Nord, which has entered the collective memory thanks to Marcel Carné. Situated on the bank of the Saint-Martin canal, the establishment has retained its famous façade since 1885, despite the numerous redevelopments the area has undergone. Having gradually fallen into disrepair, the hotel was renovated in 1993 thanks to appeals by nostalgic Parisians. Since then, its current owner has successfully met the challenge of transforming it into a fashionable venue, while retaining its history-steeped atmosphere. You enter first into the cosy bar, whose interior has a 1930s influence with its black and white checked tiled floor and zinc bar. Then, after passing through an amazing library, you're received into the intimate ambiance of the restaurant. The menu gives traditional flavours a modern twist using fresh produce, in dishes like the house *confit de canard* with ginger-honey sauce. The wine list and the abundant selection of teas from Betjeman & Barton will delight the most discerning palates.

With the exception of a few scenes, the film was shot in the studios at Boulogne-Billancourt where the Hotel du Nord was completely reconstructed.

L'HÔTEL DU NORD
-
102, quai de Jemmapes
75010 Paris
-
Ⓜ Jacques-Bonsergent
or République
-
☎ 01 40 40 78 78
www.hoteldunord.org
-
Price:
★★☆☆☆

WATCH THE TRAILER

L'ATMOSPHÈRE

location for:

RUSSIAN DOLLS

by CÉDRIC KLAPISCH

with ROMAIN DURIS, CÉCILE DE FRANCE,

AUDREY TAUTOU, KELLY REILLY, KEVIN BISHOP

• 2005 •

Kevin Bishop tells Romain Duris about his meeting with 'Natasha'

L'ATMOSPHÈRE
-
49, rue Lucien-Sampaix
75010 Paris
-
Ⓜ Gare-de-l'Est
or Jacques-Bonsergent
-
☎ 01 40 38 09 21
www.latmosphere.fr
-
Price:
★★☆☆☆

WATCH THE TRAILER

Being named after Arletty's famous line (in Hotel du Nord) demands some style: l'Atmosphère has plenty. After a rock-and-roll past, marked by legendary concerts in the mid-1980s, the bistro has come of age and is devoted to a more peaceful atmosphere. Open every day of the year, it enjoys a privileged position on the bank of the quai de Valmy, which gives it an undeniable serenity. Friends meet here in the early evening for drink on the terrace and at weekends families take a break here with children or couples come for a romantic dinner in surroundings that are conducive to intimate conversation and maybe more. Rumor has it at least twenty babies have been born of meetings at l'Atmosphère.

Delicious house-made dishes are prepared using fresh produce: fish, meat and vegetables are chosen daily. A wide selection of wines are available by the bottle, carafe or glass. And for after, leave space for generous portions of dessert.

Its lovely terrace and perfect location alongside the Saint-Martin canal gave l'Atmosphère all the ingredients necessary for it to be chosen as a location for the film.

POINT ÉPHÉMÈRE

location for:

'LOLITA' – THE PLAYERS
by ÉRIC LARTIGAU
with GILLES LELLOUCHE, JEAN DUJARDIN
• 2012 •

Gilles Lellouche buys a round for 'Lolita' and her friends

POINT ÉPHÉMÈRE
-
200, quai de Valmy
75010 Paris
-
Ⓜ Jaurès or Louis-Blanc
-
☎ 01 40 34 02 48
www.pointephemere.org
-
Price:
★☆☆☆☆

WATCH THE TRAILER

See also:
le Bombardier,
le Pure Café

Launched in 2004 by the Association Usines Éphémères (ephemeral factories association) in a hardware store, Point Éphémère has become a permanent dynamic arts centre, although it was intended to be only temporary. Today it hosts artists in spaces designed for residencies (four artists' studios, a dance studio and five music studios) and offers the public a large and diverse programme of concerts, dance, conferences, exhibitions, workshops and receptions in concert and exhibition halls that give the false impression of being disused.

In addition to the community-sharing aspect, there is a bar and a restaurant, to which people flock in summertime for the large terrace on the Saint-Martin canal quayside, away from the busy streets. The food is healthy and the prices moderate with set-price lunches during the week and brunches at weekends costing less than 15 euros. Éric Lartigau shot the short film 'Lolita' for *The Players* at the bar of this alternative venue frequented by young people from the east side of Paris. As its decor is constantly evolving, the purple walls seen in the film have since disappeared. The venue's dance studio hosted Karin Viard for a flamenco lesson in *Change of Plans*.

On Sundays from 7.30pm, Kristin, the cook, sets up her Gourmet Food Truck to sell burgers in front of Point Éphémère

L'HÔTEL KUNTZ

location for:

BELOVED

by CHRISTOPHE HONORÉ

with CHIARA MASTROIANNI, LUDIVINE SAGNIER, CATHERINE DENEUVE,

MILOS FORMAN, RASHA BUKVIC, LOUIS GARREL

• 2011 •

Stolen moments for Catherine Deneuve and Milos Forman

L'HÔTEL KUNTZ
-
2, rue des Deux-Gares
75010 Paris
-
Ⓜ Gare-de-l'Est
or Gare-du-Nord
-
☎ 01 40 37 75 29
www.hotelkuntz.com
-
Price:
★☆☆☆☆

WATCH THE TRAILER

See also:
le Cercle Clichy Montmartre,
l'Hôtel Camelia

This simple, family-sized hotel, ideally situated just a few steps from the Gare de l'Est and the Gare du Nord, offers very attractive prices if you book online.

Christophe Honoré once again set up his cameras in the Hotel Kuntz, having previously made an eponymous short film here, available only as a bonus on the DVD of his film *La Belle Personne*. This time he very sensitively filmed Catherine Deneuve and Milos Forman as lovers, in love and in hiding in their very discreet love-nest of rooms 54 and 44.

LE BRADY

location for:

LOVE SONGS

by CHRISTOPHE HONORÉ

with LUDIVINE SAGNIER, CLOTILDE HESME,

CHIARA MASTROIANNI, LOUIS GARREL

• 2007 •

Gripes about always going to the cinema alone

Opening in 1956 with the musical *Ma sœur est du tonnerre* (*My Sister Eileen*), Le Brady soon changed register to specialize in horror movies. For more than 40 years, movie-goers have been coming to seek thrills in this darkened auditorium. In 1994, Jean-Pierre Mocky took over the management and renovated the cinema to restore its original façade and build a new auditorium. Since then there have been no more horrors in the programming and Le Brady has made a name for itself with its discerning and eclectic selection of films.

LE BRADY
-
39, bd. de Strasbourg
75010 Paris
-
Ⓜ Château-d'Eau
-
☎ 01 47 70 08 86
www.lebrady.fr

Price:
★☆☆☆☆

WATCH THE TRAILER

LE PASSAGE BRADY

location for:

FRANTIC

by ROMAN POLANSKI

with HARRISON FORD, BETTY BUCKLEY, EMMANUELLE SEIGNER

• 1988 •

Harrison Ford starts searching for his missing wife

The Passage Brady is one of twenty arcades remaining in Paris. The luminosity of its glass roof gives it a unique aura. Built in 1828 for a middle-class clientele wanting shelter from bad weather while shopping, it was eventually deserted as the area became increasingly insalubrious. Then in the 1970s, M. Ponnoussamy, from Pondicherry, opened an Indian restaurant here and very quickly, Indian, Pakistani, Sri Lankan and Bangladeshi communities set up shop. And thus Little India was born. Today, shops selling spices and windows displaying saris compete for customers with their exotic flavours and vibrant colours.

At each premises, an Indian restaurant, sometimes with the backup of its rather boastful owner, invites you on a marvelous culinary voyage. Biryani, punjabi lamb curry, papadum, mysore pak and other dishes will delight your tastebuds for a very modest bill, wherever you end up.

In a nod to the film *The Legend of the Holy Drinker*, the actor Dominique Pinon again plays a Parisian tramp useful to the hero, this time under the direction of Roman Polanski.

LE PASSAGE BRADY
-
Entrance near
33, bd. de Strasbourg or
46, rue du Faubourg-Saint-Denis
75010 Paris
-
Ⓜ Château-d'Eau
or Strasbourg-Saint-Denis
-
Price:
★☆☆☆☆

WATCH THE TRAILER

JULIEN

location for:

LA VIE EN ROSE

by OLIVIER DAHAN

with MARION COTILLARD, GÉRARD DEPARDIEU,

SYLVIE TESTUD, PASCAL GREGGORY

• 2007 •

Édith Piaf calls for Champagne for her table

JULIEN
-
16, rue du Fg-Saint-Denis
75010 Paris
-
Ⓜ Strasbourg-Saint-Denis
-
☎ 01 47 70 12 06
www.julienparis.com
-
Price:
★★☆☆☆

WATCH THE TRAILER

An unexpected place is hidden away on the well-known rue du Faubourg-Saint-Denis. Once you've ventured through the mysterious curtains, a breathtaking, ageless interior offers itself up flamboyantly to your gaze: welcome to the Julien brasserie, an Art Nouveau gem. Over the years, this exceptional setting was indulged without restraint by artists: from the glass peacocks by Armand Segaud to the flower women of the master glassmaker Louis Trézel, via the sublime glass ceiling designed by Charles Buffet. Today, the place exudes calm, luxury and old-fashioned sensual pleasure.

Frequented by numerous artists, the brasserie has counted among its regulars, in particular, Edith Piaf, who would invariably sit with her friends at table 24 to wait for Marcel Cerdan, whose boxing club was nearby.

The place logically ended up as a setting for *La Vie en Rose*, particularly since nowhere else in the world could recreate the atmosphere of such a Parisian brasserie. Despite budgetary constraints, Olivier Dahan respectfully chose to film at Julien, faithfully placing Oscar-winner Marion Cotillard on the Little Sparrow's favourite banquette.

43	LE MÉCANO BAR	BAR	*LITTLE WHITE LIES*
44	AUX FOLIES	BAR	*PARIS*
45	LE ZÉPHYR	BISTRO	*CHANGE OF PLANS*
46	LA HALLE AUX OLIVIERS	RESTAURANT	*CHANGE OF PLANS*

BELLEVILLE

LE MÉCANO BAR

location for:

LITTLE WHITE LIES

by GUILLAUME CANET

with GILLES LELLOUCHE, MARION COTILLARD, FRANÇOIS CLUZET, BENOÎT MAGIMEL,

VALÉRIE BONNETON, PASCALE ARBILLOT, LAURENT LAFITTE, JEAN DUJARDIN

• 2010 •

A last dinner in Paris before leaving on holiday

Established in 1832 as a hardware store specialising in modern machinery and equipment, this space has since been transformed into a must-visit bar on the busy rue Oberkampf.

An odd contraption symbolically placed on a Chesterfield sofa, colourful walls and an assortment of chairs give the bar's interior a retro-chic style that is enhanced by its unique setting.

People come to the Mécano Bar for its party atmosphere, especially at weekends, when the bar stays open all night. The menu features simple and affordable fare with original dishes, such as an irresistible farmhouse cheeseburger with homemade chips, a chicken and farm vegetable stir-fry, or a tuna steak flamed in balsamic vinegar. If you just want a snack, the cold meat and cheese platters are a great back-to-basics option.

Guillaume Canet set his actors up in the room at the back, where the subdued lighting is more conducive to intimate conversation.

LE MÉCANO BAR
-
99, rue Oberkampf
75010 Paris
-
Ⓜ Parmentier
-
☎ 01 40 21 35 28
www.mecanobar.fr

Price:
★☆☆☆☆

WATCH THE TRAILER

See also:
Pershing Hall

AUX FOLIES

location for:

PARIS

by CÉDRIC KLAPISCH

with ROMAIN DURIS, JULIETTE BINOCHE,

MÉLANIE LAURENT, FABRICE LUCHINI, KARIN VIARD

• 2008 •

Mélanie Laurent forces Fabrice Luchini to face reality

AUX FOLIES
-
8, rue de Belleville
75020 Paris
-
Ⓜ Belleville
-
☎ 01 46 36 65 98
-
Price:
★☆☆☆☆

WATCH THE TRAILER

See also:
Villalys

It is impossible to miss this anachronistic bistro and its pink neon sign at the intersection of the busy rues Dénoyer and de Belleville.

Inside, multi-coloured neon lights on the ceiling flirt with kitsch formica tables beneath the amused gaze of the huge zinc bar and posts covered with sheet music by Lucienne Delyle and Tino Rossi. Because even today, bathed in graffiti, the bar unapologetically pays homage to its heyday as a café-théâtre, when it was frequented by such greats as Edith Piaf and Maurice Chevalier. Its neighborhood vibe is palpable in the friendly hubbub and the more heated discussions at the bar. Customers enter and leave amidst a frenzied hustle and bustle, the more indolent among them settling in on the terrace to enjoy the hectic activity of the *quartier*.

The clientele is eclectic: barflies, punters and tourists come to Aux Folies for its unique atmosphere and modest prices. You have to pay cash here: they take neither cheques nor credit cards. Cédric Klapisch filmed Mélanie Laurent in the large windows of this bistro to allow her professor Fabrice Luchini a glimpse into his young student's life, in all its transparency.

An artsy dive
ambiance with rock
and Motown playing
in the background

LE ZÉPHYR

location for:

CHANGE OF PLANS

by DANIÈLE THOMPSON

with KARIN VIARD, DANY BOON, MARINA FOÏS, PATRICK BRUEL, MARINA HANDS,

EMMANUELLE SEIGNER, CHRISTOPHER THOMPSON, PATRICK CHESNAIS

• 2009 •

Karin Viard makes two important announcements to Dany Boon

On arriving here, we looked for a spot outside to make the most of the terrace, but once through the door, we chose to stay among the wood panelling, gleaming bar, classic copper coffee-roaster, huge bevelled mirrors and garnet-coloured barquettes rich in history. The Zéphyr charm was at work. We then explored the hearty, traditional menu. Casting a quick glance at the next-door table, we spotted a beautiful steak served on a wooden platter with hand-cut chips. But they keep the best for the weekend: the 'pique-nique' brunch. In true country style, the meal is served in a lovely wicker basket filled with a tomato-mozzarella salad, sausage and chips, fried eggs served in a mini frying pan, Danish pastries, fromage blanc, jam and fruit, accompanied by a hot drink and freshly squeezed fruit juice or, for a few euros extra, a glass of Champagne.

It's hardly surprising that film crews have followed each other to this location: the unspoiled 1930s bistro adds an extra special something to each film's atmosphere.

LE ZÉPHYR
-
1, rue du Jourdain
75020 Paris
-
Ⓜ Jourdain

☎ 01 46 36 65 81
www.lezephyrcafe.com

Price:
★★☆☆☆
WATCH THE TRAILER

See also:
les Ombres, le Pure Café,
la Halle aux Oliviers,
le marché Maubert,
Point Éphémère

LA HALLE AUX OLIVIERS

location for:

CHANGE OF PLANS

by DANIÈLE THOMPSON

with KARIN VIARD, DANY BOON, MARINA FOÏS, PATRICK BRUEL, MARINA HANDS,

EMMANUELLE SEIGNER, CHRISTOPHER THOMPSON, PATRICK CHESNAIS

• 2009 •

*A year later, Karin Viard gets her friends
together for the Fête de la Musique*

**LA HALLE
AUX OLIVIERS**
-
19-21, rue Boyer
75020 Paris
-
Ⓜ Gambetta or Ménilmontant
-
☎ 01 46 36 07 07
www.labellevilloise.com
-
Price:
★★☆☆☆

WATCH THE TRAILER

See also:
les Ombres, le Pure Café,
le Zéphyr, Point Éphémère,
le marché Maubert

In 1877, at the initiative of some twenty workers, a small cooperative grocery warehouse was opened. Over the years, the place played an important role in the economic and cultural life of the east side of Paris, enabling those on a low income to benefit from a political education and culture, and also experimented with fair trading between producers and consumers. Today, having become La Bellevilloise, it is affectionately and appropriately known as the 'cultural fortress', offering an independent venue for artistic activities and events (concerts, shows, exhibitions, clubbing...) as well as a restaurant, La Halle aux Oliviers. On the terrace or in the winter garden, planted with hundred-year-old olive trees, you can enjoy original and understated food in a relaxed atmosphere. And to brighten up your weekend, there's a Jazz Brunch on Sundays.

Danièle Thompson chose La Halle aux Oliviers as the setting for the final flamenco-rhythmed scene of her film.

The bar serves a variety of cocktails alongside the restaurant

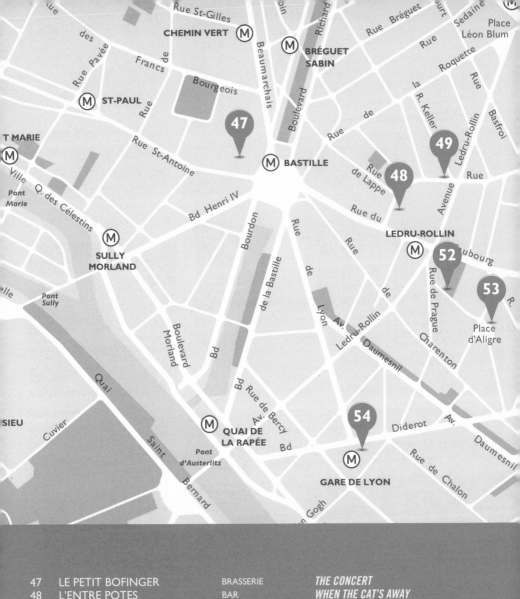

47	LE PETIT BOFINGER	BRASSERIE	*THE CONCERT*
48	L'ENTRE POTES	BAR	*WHEN THE CAT'S AWAY*
49	LE PAUSE CAFÉ	BISTRO	*WHEN THE CAT'S AWAY*
50	LE PURE CAFÉ	BISTRO	*BEFORE SUNSET*
51	AU VIEUX CHÊNE	BISTRO	*I'VE BEEN WAITING SO LONG*
52	LE SQUARE TROUSSEAU	BRASSERIE	*LE PÈRE NOËL EST UNE ORDURE*
53	LE MARCHÉ D'ALIGRE	SHOP	*'BASTILLE' – PARIS, I LOVE YOU*
54	LE TRAIN BLEU	RESTAURANT	*LA FEMME NIKITA*

BASTILLE

LE PETIT BOFINGER

location for:

THE CONCERT

by RADU MIHAILEANU

with MÉLANIE LAURENT, ALEXEÏ GOUSKOV, DIMITRI NAZAROV, FRANÇOIS BERLÉAND

• 2009 •

A Bolshoi musician tries to palm off
his caviar on the restaurateur

LE PETIT
BOFINGER
-
6, rue de la Bastille
75011 Paris
-
Ⓜ Bastille
-
☎ 01 42 72 05 23
www.bofingerparis.com
-
Price:
★★★☆☆

WATCH THE TRAILER

The story of Bofinger is a story of family. The original, established since 1864 near the Bastille, was founded by Colmar-native Frédéric Bofinger, who decided to make it the first Parisian brasserie to serve draught beer. Since then, the place with the sumptuous Art Nouveau decor has become a deservedly successful institution with a discerning and often famous clientele: François Mitterrand chose to celebrate his move into the Elysée Palace here on 10 May 1981 and the brasserie hosted Polnareff's first night out after his return to France. On the strength of this success, the brasserie's prodigal son, Petit Bofinger, was born just across the street, with the goal of preserving the same excellent standard of cuisine at mid-range prices aimed at a more laid-back, family clientele in surroundings true to the Belle Époque style. The set menus include a succulent traditional sauerkraut served with meats of superb quality.

The authority of the chef in his toque, in the setting of this typically French restaurant, contrasts perfectly with the Russian musician trying to sell his caviar on the black market from a cardboard suitcase.

L'ENTRE POTES

location for:

WHEN THE CAT'S AWAY

by CÉDRIC KLAPISCH

with GARANCE CLAVEL, ZINEDINE SOUALEM, ROMAIN DURIS

• 1996 •

Romain Duris can't get close to Garance Clavel

L'ENTRE POTES
-
14, rue de Charonne
75011 Paris
-
Ⓜ Ledru-Rollin
-
☎ 01 48 06 57 04
-
Price:
★☆☆☆☆

See also:
le Pause Café

A former coal warehouse, Entre Potes is an evening bar that is secretly guarded by its faithful regulars. We came here initially just to have a drink, but were soon captivated by this unreal place. With its 'underground' outward appearance, weatherbeaten old bar, and graffiti and yesteryear posters on the walls, Entre Potes is to all appearances an old-fashioned place. On the ground floor, facing the long galvanized bar, a huge painted fresco sets the tone. But like Alice, we then entered a wonderland, passing bistro chairs and a timeless cream leather sofa to discover a real patio backed up against a fake house, finally arriving in a hidden-away, cosy square of banquettes. In the basement, we beamed with pleasure at the surprise of finding ourselves inside an impressively realistic reconstruction of a metro station, including an intimate alcove, which is reserved for private parties.

Cédric Klapisch brought the place into the spotlight and it was later Edouard Baer's turn to camp out at Entre Potes for his live broadcast, *Secrets de femme*, transmitted on Paris Première and Radio Nova.

In the heydey of the Palace nightclub, legend has it that Prince organized unforgettable evenings here after his shows

LE PAUSE CAFÉ

location for:

WHEN THE CAT'S AWAY

by CÉDRIC KLAPISCH

with GARANCE CLAVEL, ZINEDINE SOUALEM, ROMAIN DURIS

• 1996 •

Garance Clavel asks Renée Le Calm about her cat

Just a pause café (coffee break)? No, take the time to sit down and you'll be loathe to budge from this bistro in the heart of Bastille that Didier, its owner for the past twenty years, has decorated in the fashion of an idealized New York eatery. A white brick wall beneath a high ceiling, an enormous station clock and hanging slate menus complete the illusion perfectly. Dreamers on bicycles, the *quartier*'s stylish youth and laid-back celebrities out to have a good time crowd onto the sunny terrace with regulars to enjoy simple and accessible dishes all day long in a friendly atmosphere.

A friend of Cédric Klapisch's, Didier lent him Pause Café on a Monday when the café was closed to save him shooting expenses on what was at that stage a low-budget short film. A few years and much success later, *When the Cat's Away* was exported and it's not uncommon to spot American and Japanese visitors crossing the threshold of Pause Café for the pleasure of seeing a place they had first discovered in their arthouse cinemas on the other side of the world.

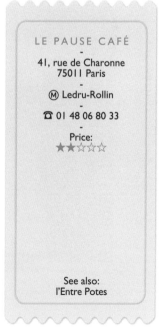

LE PAUSE CAFÉ
-
41, rue de Charonne
75011 Paris
-
Ⓜ Ledru-Rollin
-
☎ 01 48 06 80 33
-
Price:
★★☆☆☆
-

See also:
l'Entre Potes

LE PURE CAFÉ

location for:

BEFORE SUNSET

by RICHARD LINKLATER

with JULIE DELPY, ETHAN HAWKE

• 2005 •

A heart-to-heart for Julie Delpy and Ethan Hawke

LE PURE CAFÉ
-
14, rue Jean-Macé
75011 Paris
-
Ⓜ Charonne
or Faidherbe-Chaligny
-
☎ 01 43 71 47 22
www.purecafe.fr
-
Price:
★★☆☆☆

WATCH THE TRAILER

See also:
Shakespeare and Company

There's a vintage-chic ambiance about this bistro with its old-fashioned sign, rocket lamps, mosaic tiled floor and imposing old galvanized bar that's perfect for enjoying a good glass of wine. The large bay windows encircling the room make it a lovely and bright alternative to the terrace that is open all year round. The menu offers simple yet sophisticated dishes in a casual, friendly setting.

Thanks to its privileged location away from the area's hustle and bustle, Le Pure Café has hosted many international film shoots. Among the most famous, is that of *Before Sunset*, which reunited Julie Delpy and Ethan Hawke for a day in Paris, but also an episode of the cult series *ER*, which brought Noah Wyle to Paris. Since then, it is not uncommon to run into American tourists at Le Pure Café. Of course, French directors are not to be left out: Danièle Thompson leaned on the bar next to Dany Boon for coffee and a croissant in *Change of Plans* and Jean Dujardin speculated with Gilles Lellouche over a beer on the terrace in the first sketch of the film *The Players*.

AU VIEUX CHÊNE

location for:

I'VE BEEN WAITING SO LONG

by THIERRY KLIFA

with NATHALIE BAYE, PATRICK BRUEL, GÉRALDINE PAILHAS

• 2004 •

Patrick Bruel, Anouck Grinberg and Michaël Cohen's restaurant

AU VIEUX CHÊNE
-
7, rue du Dahomey
75011 Paris
-
Ⓜ Faidherbe-Chaligny
or Charonne
-
☎ 01 43 71 67 69
www.vieuxchene.fr
-
Price:
★★☆☆☆

Hidden away behind the busy Faubourg Saint-Antoine, Au Vieux Chêne is a little gem of a bistro overflowing with charm and simplicity. Managed in the 1930s by a wood craftsman, who named it Au Vieux Chêne in tribute to the tree of the area's cabinetmakers, for a long time it remained a modest canteen for local factory workers. It's now more sought out by the new clientele of the Faubourg Saint-Antoine and its food is deliciously sophisticated. For all that, however, the restaurant hasn't put on airs and graces, as can been seen in its decor, which has retained the authenticity of its brick wall and classic tiling, not to mention the friendly hospitality of its owner. The dishes focus on high-quality produce, each ingredient being chosen with respect for small farmers. The same discernment applies to the wine list, which offers over 150 wines made by independent winemakers. Au Vieux Chêne provided just the cosy, intimate setting that Thierry Klifa was looking for, its warm, unaffected atmosphere enabling him to dramatize the shared moments in the lives of the film's three restaurant owners, Patrick Bruel, Anouck Grinberg and Michaël Cohen.

LE SQUARE TROUSSEAU

location for:

LE PÈRE NOËL EST UNE ORDURE

by JEAN-MARIE POIRÉ

with ANÉMONE, THIERRY LHERMITTE, MARIE-ANNE CHAZEL, GÉRARD JUGNOT

• 1982 •

Zézette and Thérèse perk up with a drink at the bar

**LE SQUARE
TROUSSEAU**
-
1, rue Antoine-Vollon
75012 Paris
-
Ⓜ Ledru-Rollin
-
☎ 01 43 43 06 00
www.squaretrousseau.com
-
Price:
★★☆☆☆

Bordering the square for the past hundred years, the restaurant has miraculously retained its Art Nouveau decor. Stucco mouldings, antiquated photographs in gilded wooden frames, moleskin banquettes and heavy red velvet curtains compete in splendour. Proud of its grandeur, the sumptuous wood and zinc bar steals the show. And the service is on a par: white tablecloths and napkins and logotype glasses and plates greet the gourmet diner. In this yesteryear environment, the menu offers revisited traditional cuisine: the prawn risotto and a bowl of chocolate mousse to share kept us in silent enjoyment for several minutes. Noteworthy, too, is the interesting and affordable wine list. For a more intimate setting, a very elegant private dining room, like that of an upscale townhouse, can be booked for up to eighteen people around an impeccably set table. Finally, the restaurant's annex sells regional products and fine, sought-after wines.

Jean Gabin was a regular at Le Square Trousseau, but it was our own Zézette and Thérèse who inspired our affection for this wonderful place.

LE MARCHÉ D'ALIGRE

location for:

'BASTILLE' – PARIS, I LOVE YOU

by ISABEL COIXET

with SERGIO CASTELLITTO, MIRANDA RICHARDSON

• 2006 •

The man catches sight of the red raincoat

Fruits and vegetables, spices and bric-a-brac – a world of colours and fragrances awaits you on a baroque square with an atmosphere that is second to none. Established in the eighteenth century a stone's throw from the Bastille, which at the time was a working-class neighbourhood, this unique market has remained popular over the years in part because prices are lower here than anywhere else in Paris. The Aligre market has also become a symbol of diversity: today, it is frequented by all social classes, while on the other side of the stalls, traders from all over the world offer goods that are hard to find in France. A highlight of this exceptional place is the flea market, where you can hunt for bargains without breaking the bank. Finally, bordering the square is the very chic Halle Beauvau, home to butchers, charcutiers, fishmongers, cheesemongers and delicatessens. In fine weather, take time to stop for a drink on the terrace of one of the many neighbouring bistros or at a makeshift bar selling wine unpretentiously from the barrel. Isabel Coixet magically chose the hustle and bustle of the Aligre Market to give the man hope again.

LE MARCHÉ
D'ALIGRE
-
Place d'Aligre
75011 Paris
-
Ⓜ Ledru-Rollin
-
Price:
★☆☆☆☆

WATCH THE TRAILER

LE TRAIN BLEU

location for:

LA FEMME NIKITA

by LUC BESSON

with ANNE PARILLAUD, TCHÉKY KARYO, JEAN-HUGUES ANGLADE,

JEANNE MOREAU, JEAN RENO, JEAN BOVISE

• 1990 •

Nikita celebrates her birthday

LE TRAIN BLEU
-
Place Louis-Armand
First floor of the Gare de Lyon
75012 Paris
-
Ⓜ Gare-de-Lyon
-
☎ 01 43 43 09 06
www.le-train-bleu.com
-
Price:
★★★★☆

WATCH THE TRAILER

See also:
le Club de tir de Paris
de la Police nationale

Built along with the station for the 1900 World's Fair by the French railway company Paris-Lyon-Méditerranée (PLM), Le Train Bleu was at the time humbly *called the Buffet de la gare de Lyon*. It took its present-day name in 1963 in tribute to the legendary and luxurious Paris-Ventimiglia train. Although its façade is fairly modest for the Belle Epoque, once you're inside this restaurant, which is housed on the first floor of the station, you're suddenly overwhelmed by its splendid, spectacular opulence: three huge rooms rival each other in the extravagance of their gilding and mouldings, but most impressive are the forty-one colourful frescoes on the walls and ceilings, which retrace the landscapes of yesteryear traversed by the company's trains. The restaurant serves traditional and refined cuisine that is a culinary sensation, while uniformed service, white table linen and logotype crockery add the final solicitous and sumptuous flourish. Many celebrities have crossed its threshold over the years, including Coco Chanel, Salvador Dalí and François Mitterrand.

Luc Besson marked his territory by destroying the restaurant under the intense and apocalyptic fire of Anne Parillaud playing an unforgettable Nikita.

55	AU MARCHÉ DE LA BUTTE	SHOP	*AMÉLIE*
56	LE MANÈGE DU SACRÉ-CŒUR	EXPERIENCE	*ITINÉRAIRE D'UN ENFANT GÂTÉ*
57	LE FUNICULAIRE DE MONTMARTRE	EXPERIENCE	*A MONSTER IN PARIS*
58	STUDIO 28	CULTURE	*AMÉLIE*
59	LE CAFÉ DES 2 MOULINS	BISTRO	*AMÉLIE*
60	LE MOULIN ROUGE	CULTURE	*MOULIN ROUGE!*
61	LA BOULANGERIE DU MOULIN DE LA GALETTE	SHOP	*JULIE & JULIA*
62	LA RESNAISSANCE	BISTRO	*INGLOURIOUS BASTERDS*
63	TIN-TIN TATOUEUR	EXPERIENCE	*DÉPRESSION ET DES POTES*
64	LE CERCLE CLICHY MONTMARTRE	EXPERIENCE	*BELOVED*
65	L'HÔTEL CAMÉLIA	HOTEL	*TAKEN*

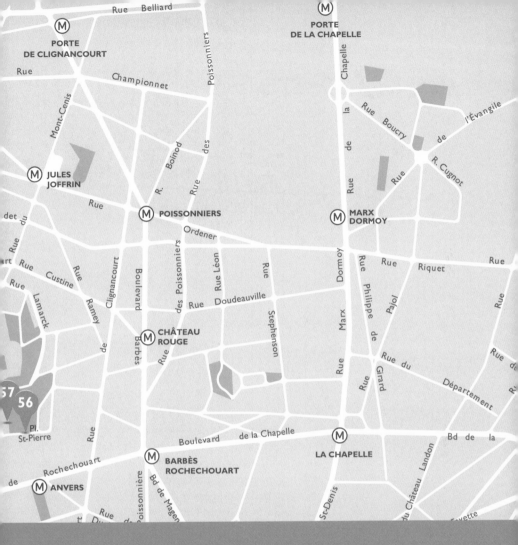

MONTMARTRE

AU MARCHÉ DE LA BUTTE

location for:

AMÉLIE

by JEAN-PIERRE JEUNET

with AUDREY TAUTOU, MATHIEU KASSOVITZ, ISABELLE NANTY

• 2001 •

Amélie puts down Collignon

AU MARCHÉ
DE LA BUTTE
-
56, rue des Trois-Frères
75018 Paris
-
Ⓜ Abbesses
-
☎ 01 42 64 86 30
-
Price:
★☆☆☆☆

WATCH THE TRAILER

See also:
le Café des 2 Moulins,
le Verre à pied, Studio 28

We feel a rush of emotion facing Au Marché de la Butte and it's with great joy that we find ourselves standing in front of Amélie's legendary grocery store, which comes to life before our eyes. The shop's owner, Ali, is indeed a clever magician who has managed to preserve the decor and make real the unforgettable atmosphere of the film. From the gleaming green shop front, the 'Maison Collignon' wrought-iron sign and the garden gnomes at the entrance to the twin fruit and vegetable stands outside, nothing is missing, except perhaps some accordion music to give us the urge to listen to the whispers of his endives. Finally, to reassure the suspicious tourist, Ali has filled a window with press cuttings paying tribute to his humble shop, which has become an enduring cult spot for film lovers worldwide. We were able to resist neither the full postcard spinner rack nor the original film soundtrack sold at the counter. And in order to enjoy the place a while longer, we also stocked up on provisions of biscuits and soft drinks for our rambles. After all, people come chez Collignon to do their shopping too.

The most photographed grocery store in Paris

LE MANÈGE DU SACRÉ-CŒUR

location for:

ITINÉRAIRE D'UN ENFANT GÂTÉ

by CLAUDE LELOUCH

with JEAN-PAUL BELMONDO, RICHARD ANCONINA

• 1988 •

Little Sam is abandoned by his mother

LE MANÈGE DU SACRÉ-CŒUR
-
Square Louise-Michel
75018 Paris
-
Ⓜ Abbesses
-
Price:
★☆☆☆☆

Like a postcard at the foot of Sacré-Cœur, the Montmartre merry-go-round is at the top of the list of the most beautiful carousels in Paris, along with those at the Trocadéro, the Tuileries and the Jardin des plantes. Made in Italy and family-run from the start, this multi-coloured double-decker hurly-burly of wooden horses welcomes children and adults on board every day of the year.

Claude Lelouch, who holds Montmartre dear, chose to use it at the beginning of *Itinéraire d'un enfant gâté* to show the hero being abandoned into the hands of fairground people.

LE FUNICULAIRE DE MONTMARTRE

location for:

A MONSTER IN PARIS

by ÉRIC BERGERON

with les voix de VANESSA PARADIS, M

• 2011 •

Francœur escapes on the funicular railway with the help of a monkey

Built in 1900, the Montmartre funicular railway, today managed by the RATP, connects Pigalle and Montmartre for the price of a single metro ticket and drops off more than two million travelers a year at the foot of Sacré-Cœur. Its glass cabins climb thirty-six metres in less than a minute and a half, bypassing the 222 steps, which it leaves to the more courageous. More of an attraction than a means of transport, the funicular railway has been featured in many films, including *A Monster in Paris*, where it provides the setting for the final battle.

LE FUNICULAIRE
DE MONTMARTRE

-

Place Suzanne-Valandon
75018 Paris

-

Ⓜ Abbesses

-

www.ratp.fr

-

Price:
★☆☆☆☆

WATCH THE TRAILER

See also:
les grandes serres
du jardin des Plantes

STUDIO 28

location for:

AMÉLIE

by JEAN-PIERRE JEUNET

with AUDREY TAUTOU, MATHIEU KASSOVITZ, ISABELLE NANTY

• 2001 •

The cinema frequented by Amélie Poulain

STUDIO 28
-
10, rue Tholozé
75018 Paris
-
Ⓜ Blanche or Abbesses
-
☎ 01 46 06 36 07
www.cinemastudio28.com
-
Price:
★☆☆☆☆

WATCH THE TRAILER

See also:
le Café des 2 Moulins,
le Verre à pied,
au marché de la Butte

Since its opening in 1928, this arthouse cinema of the village of Montmartre has endeavoured to discover young filmmakers and to offer quality films, from Buñuel's banned L'Âge d'Or to the Marx Brothers' comedies, from 'intimist' treasures to the latest classics. Although Studio 28 is the oldest cinema still operating in Paris, it has kept up with the times, equipping itself with a digital Sony 4K projection room, Dolby Digital 5.1 and 7.1 Surround Sound and air conditioning, while retaining its old-world charm with chandeliers designed by its patron Jean Cocteau. The red carpet painted onto the steps provides a touch of elegance, while on the foyer walls you can admire casts of the footprints of such legendary actors as Jeanne Moreau and Jean Marais before heading into a long corridor that offers a new exhibition every month. Finally, everything is designed to satisfy the desire for conversation, for discussing a film over a drink at the bar or while having a bite to eat in the garden.

Jean-Pierre Jeunet couldn't shoot *Amélie*, an ode to Montmartre, without incorporating this extraordinary cinema, the essence of what makes Montmartre unique.

LE CAFÉ DES 2 MOULINS

location for:

AMÉLIE

by JEAN-PIERRE JEUNET

with AUDREY TAUTOU, MATHIEU KASSOVITZ, ISABELLE NANTY

• 2001 •

Audrey Tautou is a waitress at the Café des 2 Moulins

Regulars are not mistaken in sharing with tourists their neighbourhood bistro with its atmosphere of times gone by, for today it has become a true Parisian star. Indeed, while the cigarette counter at which Isabelle Nanty toiled has disappeared, the green and red ambiance of the film is no longer to be found, and the bar and a poster are the only witnesses to Jean-Pierre Jeunet's brief presence here, the café can pride itself on being, since Amélie, a Parisian icon for film lovers from all over the world. While curious sightseers continue to pose for pictures in front of the windows, tourist obsession does nothing to detract from the warm simplicity of this traditional café, whose name pays tribute to the two windmills nearby: the Moulin Rouge and the Moulin de la Galette. Its classic, old-fashioned Parisian cooking is much appreciated and the service is efficient.

Finally, a terrace open all day long allows you to watch the goings-on of the very busy rue Lepic, and is particularly good for Sunday brunch when the weather is fine.

Whether as a cinematic icon or simply a good bistro, the Café des 2 Moulins continues to get top billing.

LE CAFÉ
DES 2 MOULINS
-
15, rue Lepic
75018 Paris
-
Ⓜ Blanche
-
☎ 01 42 54 90 50

Price:
★★☆☆☆

WATCH THE TRAILER

See also:
Studio 28, le Verre à pied,
au marché de la Butte

LE MOULIN ROUGE

location for:

MOULIN ROUGE !

de BAZ LUHRMANN

avec NICOLE KIDMAN, EWAN MCGREGOR

• 2001 •

Ewan McGregor succumbs to Nicole Kidman's charms

LE MOULIN ROUGE
-
82, bd. de Clichy
75018 Paris
-
Ⓜ Blanche
-
☎ 01 53 09 82 82
www.moulinrouge.fr

Price:
★★★★★

WATCH THE TRAILER

The most famous cabaret in the world opened in 1889 in a then rather tawdry Montmartre where people came to slum it. Immortalized by Toulouse-Lautrec, the Moulin Rouge has inspired many films, including an eponymous one by John Huston and Jean Renoir's *French Cancan* with Jean Gabin. With its Belle Epoque decor and the feathers and sequins that adorn the national cancan, the venue is rarely taken over by film crews. So Baz Luhrmann, bewitched by this historic institution, reproduced it in its entirety in a studio.

LA BOULANGERIE DU MOULIN DE LA GALETTE

location for:

JULIE & JULIA

by NORA EPHRON

wth MERYL STREEP, AMY ADAMS, STANLEY TUCCI, CHRIS MESSINA

• 2009 •

Meryl Streep comes to buy a baguette

It's impossible to walk past this listed *boulangerie* without stopping. The cakes and pastries displayed in the window make your mouth water, urging you to push open the door into an interior whose old-fashioned tiling and painted ceiling enhance the pastries. For the purposes of the film, the crew recreated the breads and cakes of the 1950s in careful detail. Meryl Streep made the most of each break between shots to acquaint herself with *la pâtisserie française*, admitting a weakness for the succulent chouquettes.

LA BOULANGERIE
DU MOULIN
DE LA GALETTE
-
48, rue Caulaincourt
75018 Paris
-
Ⓜ Lamarck-Caulaincourt
-
☎ 01 46 06 96 71
-
Price:
★☆☆☆☆

WATCH THE TRAILER

See also:
Shakespeare and Company

LA RENAISSANCE

location for:

INGLOURIOUS BASTERDS

by QUENTIN TARANTINO

with MÉLANIE LAURENT, BRAD PITT, CHRISTOPH WALTZ

• 2009 •

Mélanie Laurent discovers that Daniel Brühl is the hero of a Nazi propaganda film

This timeless bistro has retained all of its authenticity. From the Art Deco lamp designed by Lemière to the bevelled, spotted mirrors that we so love, everything has remained as it was in the 1930s. While the splendid white marble bar invites you to lean your elbows on it, the cushiony red banquettes of the back room will captivate you most of all. At first glance, you'll quickly understand why this hidden gem attracts a good number of regulars: the traditional cuisine is in perfect keeping with the genuine refinement of the place. The menu is full of no-fuss but tasty dishes, all with that homemade touch. Wine-lovers should note that there's also a good wine list featuring reasonably priced bottles.

Quentin Tarantino chose to film Mélanie Laurent here for *Inglourious Basterds* – the only scene he shot in Paris – after discovering the bistro in Claude Chabrol's *The Blood of Others*. In all, more than ten feature films have been shot here. Topping the list are Claude Zidi with *Ripoux 1 and 2* and *Stuntwoman* with Jean-Paul Belmondo.

LA RENAISSANCE
-
112, rue Championnet
75018 Paris
-
Ⓜ Jules-Joffrin
or Porte-de-Clignancourt
-
☎ 01 46 06 01 76
www.bistrotlarenaissance.fr
-
Price:
★★☆☆☆

WATCH THE TRAILER

TIN-TIN TATOUEUR

location for:

DÉPRESSION ET DES POTES

by ARNAUD LEMORT

with FRED TESTOT, JONATHAN LAMBERT, ARIÉ ELMALEH,

ARY ABITTAN, LAURENCE ARNE

• 2012 •

Fred Testot wants to prove his love with a tattoo

TIN-TIN
TATOUEUR
-
37, rue de Douai
75009 Paris
-
Ⓜ Blanche
-
☎ 01 40 23 07 90
www.tin-tin-tattoos.com
-
Price:
★★★★★

WATCH THE TRAILER

You don't need to be a rock star or a millionaire to get a tattoo at Tin-Tin: the studio is open to everyone. Indeed, despite its much-deserved reputation over the last twenty years as one of the best tattoo parlours in the world, the prices have stayed very reasonable given the quality of the designs and the irreproachable standards of hygiene. Only the waiting time can be discouraging: it takes at least three months to get an appointment. The master and his artists are serious and passionate about their work. They will take the time, for example – rare with tattoo artists – to discuss the why and how of the illustrations and to make sure you understand the indelibility of the work. The quasi-surgical work then takes place in an ambiance where jokes help to ease the fear and the pain. Tin-Tin, a man with a strong character, chooses his own clients depending on demand and entrusts the rest to his very gifted pupils. Many celebrities, including Jean-Paul Gaultier and Joey Starr have had tattoos done here and Fred Testot, playing a hesitant depressive, couldn't but lose heart faced with a larger than life Tin-Tin in this film by Arnaud Lemort.

*The Cercle
also has the popular
multicolour roulette*

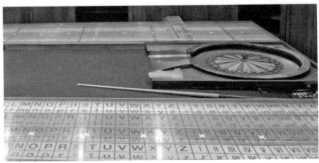

LE CERCLE CLICHY MONTMARTRE

location for:

BELOVED

by CHRISTOPHE HONORÉ

with CHIARA MASTROIANNI, LUDIVINE SAGNIER, CATHERINE DENEUVE,

MILOS FORMAN, RASHA BUKVIC

• 2011 •

Rasha Bukvic questions Ludivine Sagnier about their daugther

An old soup kitchen turned billiard hall and gaming club in 1947, the Cercle Clichy Montmartre is known by billiard and poker lovers throughout the word for its many competitions. But with just an ID card to prove you're of legal age and thirty euros for the annual membership, you can enter this gaming temple all year round and all night long, provided you've changed your torn jeans or tracksuit for proper attire.

The retro-style billiard hall offers seasoned fanatics three French billiard tables, eight American ones, a pool table and a snooker table. This little Vegas also excels with its poker tables, from Texas Hold-em to Poker 21 via Three Card Poker and Stud Poker, and tournaments are organized every week. For febrile fans fearing a bad hand or a miscue on the pristine blue cloth, there's a convivial bar that knows how to treat its customers well. Jean-Paul Belmondo settled his scores here at the end of Le Marginal and Christophe Honoré, taken by this timeless place, chose to film Ludivine Sagnier and her lover Rasha Bukvic in song here.

LE CERCLE CLICHY MONTMARTRE
-
84, rue de Clichy
75009 Paris
-
Ⓜ Place-de-Clichy
-
☎ 01 48 78 32 85
www.cerclecm.com
-
Price:
★★★☆☆

WATCH THE TRAILER

See also:
l'hôtel Kuntz, l'hôtel Camelia

L'HÔTEL CAMÉLIA

location for:

TAKEN

by PIERRE MOREL

with LIAM NEESON, MAGGIE GRACE, FAMKE JANSSEN

• 2008 •

*Liam Neeson looks after a prostitute
who is wearing his missing daughter's jacket*

L'HÔTEL CAMÉLIA
-
3, rue Darcet
75017 Paris
-
Ⓜ Place-de-Clichy
-
☎ 01 45 22 50 53
www.hotelcameliaparis.com
-
Price:
★☆☆☆☆

WATCH THE TRAILER

The nickname 'Lady of the Camellias' given to the character of Marguerite Gautier, was inspired by the life of the courteous courtesan Marie Duplessis, mistress of Alexandre Dumas the younger, to whom he paid tribute in his famous novel. According to legend, she stayed here in what was then but a humble boarding house, and today has become a charming little neighbourhood hotel. The Hotel Camelia, with its thirty rooms, with no frills but each equipped with TV and private bathroom, is situated just a few steps from the Moulin Rouge and Pigalle. Guests come here for a cheap holiday in the vibrant heart of the capital. And, because of its typically Parisian style, the hotel is regularly chosen as a location by the film world.

The reception are was monopolized for an entire night for Taken. Moreover, an eponymous title – 'Hôtel Camélia' – is found on the film's original soundtrack.

Christophe Honoré set up his film-shoot HQ here for *Beloved*. Ludivine Sagnier meets up with her lover Rasha Bukvic in the privacy of room 41. Don't forget to glance at the blue door across from the hotel, another symbolic location for the same film...

The fourth-floor rooms overlooking the street each have a small balcony

PRIX DES CHAMBRES
"HOTEL DE TOURISME"

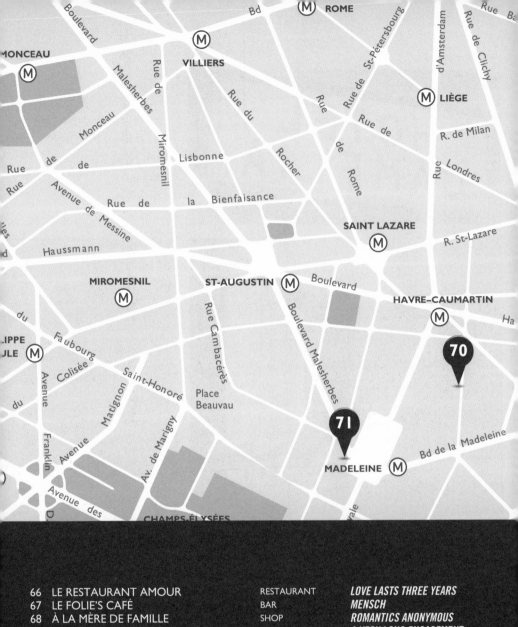

66	LE RESTAURANT AMOUR	RESTAURANT	*LOVE LASTS THREE YEARS*
67	LE FOLIE'S CAFÉ	BAR	*MENSCH*
68	À LA MÈRE DE FAMILLE	SHOP	*ROMANTICS ANONYMOUS*
69	LE BOUILLON CHARTIER	BISTRO	*A VERY LONG ENGAGEMENT*
70	ATHÉNÉE THÉÂTRE LOUIS-JOUVET	CULTURE	*HUGO*
71	SENDERENS	RESTAURANT	*HEREAFTER*

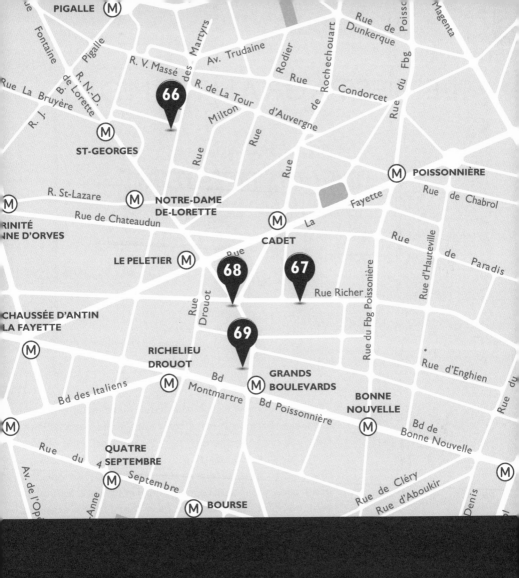

OPÉRA
TRINITÉ

LE RESTAURANT AMOUR

location for:

LOVE LASTS THREE YEARS

by FRÉDÉRIC BEIGBEDER

with LOUISE BOURGOIN, GASPARD PROUST, JOEYSTARR, VALÉRIE LEMERCIER,

JONATHAN LAMBERT, FRÉDÉRIQUE BEL

• 2012 •

Gaspard Proust replays the scene of his reunion with Louise Bourgoin

---

LE RESTAURANT AMOUR
-
8, rue Navarin
75009 Paris
-
Ⓜ Saint-Georges or Pigalle
-
☎ 01 48 78 31 80
www.hotelamourparis.fr
-
Price:
★★☆☆☆

See also:
le café de Flore

The Restaurant Amour in the hotel of the same evocative name is a charming place, a real haven in the heart of Paris. Here you can enjoy the early summer sunshine, while relaxing in the idyllic surroundings of a secret garden. Moreover, a large glass roof was recently installed to provide the seduction of the open sky all year round. Hidden in the back, four tables await romantic tête-à-têtes or more intimate conversations. The dining room, the walls of which are decorated with a collection of photographs by Terry Richardson, is in a retro 1950s Bistro style with wide red banquettes and large convivial tables, making this a great spot to share with friends. The food is nothing fancy: macaroni cheese with ham, or free-range corn-fed chicken and green or herb salad for those trying to watch their weight. For dessert, the restaurant depends on local artisans such as the famous pâtissier Delmontel.

This highly coveted place has become a must for Parisian trendies and simply had to appear in the credits of a film about the romantic relationships of nocturnal man-about-town Frédéric Beigbeder.

LE FOLIE'S CAFÉ

location for:

MENSCH

by STEVE SUISSA

with NICOLAS CAZALÉ, SARA MARTINS, ANTHONY DELON,

SAMI FREY, MAURICE BÉNICHOU

• 2009 •

Nicolas Cazalé conducts business

LE FOLIE'S CAFÉ
-
16, rue Geoffroy-Marie
75009 Paris
-
Ⓜ Cadet
-
☎ 01 48 24 04 91
www.foliescafe.fr

Price:
★★☆☆☆

Having clapped and cheered and shouted 'Encore' at the end of a show at the Folies Bergère, hungry and thirsty nightlifers often cross the street to continue their enjoyable evening out at the Folie's Café. In modern, cosy surroundings, the velvet-upholstered chairs and thick chocolate-coloured drapes invite you to luxuriate between the stone walls and the large well-stocked bar, as fitting club music plays in the background. The attentive staff serves inventive cocktails, delicious fresh-fruit smoothies and bistro fare with an Italian focus: the menu includes Milanese veal cutlets, bruschetta and tiramisu alongside more traditional brasserie dishes such as snails, tartare and lemon tart.

The neighbourhood's unique ambiance is so dear to Steve Suissa that he shot almost all the scenes for *Mensch* between rue Richer and rue de Châteaudun. And, in order to immerse himself in his director's roots, Nicolas Cazalé lived here for nearly two months of shooting and became a regular at Folie's Café.

À LA MÈRE DE FAMILLE

location for:

ROMANTICS ANONYMOUS

by JEAN-PIERRE AMÉRIS

with ISABELLE CARRÉ, BENOÎT POELVOORDE

• 2010 •

Benoît Poelvoorde finds comfort in chocolate

À LA MÈRE
DE FAMILLE
-
35, rue du Fg-Montmartre
75009 Paris
-
Ⓜ Le-Peletier
-
☎ 01 47 70 83 69
www.lameredefamille.com
-
Price:
★★☆☆☆

WATCH THE TRAILER

See also:
Legrand Filles & Fils

Originally a grocery store that opened in 1761, À la mère de famille has become a gourmet institution. This traditional shop, with two centuries of savoir-faire, hand makes all sorts of wonderful creations that will make you swoon with pleasure. The wooden shelves and counters display a mixture of chocolates, pralines, nougat, candied fruit, marshmallows and marrons glacés. Old-fashioned sweets such as hard caramels and humbugs will be a journey back into childhood for the more nostalgic. Regional specialities, such as *bêtises de Cambrai* (boiled sweets), *calissons d'Aix* (candied fruit paste) and *sablés de Nançay* (shortbread biscuits) are also highlighted. This fine place also makes its own ice cream, with a range of exquisite flavours, as well as original creations for Easter and Christmas, and suggestions for delicious luxury gifts. Although this shop is classified as an historic monument, other less distinctive but equally mouthwatering branches have opened up elsewhere in the capital.

The director chose the magical setting of Paris' oldest chocolate shop to film the chocolaty solace of romantic Benoît Poelvoorde.

LE BOUILLON CHARTIER

location for:

A VERY LONG ENGAGEMENT

by JEAN-PIERRE JEUNET

with AUDREY TAUTOU, GASPARD ULLIEL, DOMINIQUE PINON, CLOVIS CORNILLAC,
MARION COTILLARD, JEAN-PIERRE DARROUSSIN, ALBERT DUPONTEL, JEAN-PAUL ROUVE

• 2004 •

Jodie Foster has an intimate lunch with 'Bastoche'

Hidden away in a courtyard, this bistro, known simply as Le Bouillon until 1896, has lost nothing of its vocation for serving quality dishes at a modest price, such as the 'one-euro soup' in winter, and takes good care of its customers to earn their loyalty. After more than a hundred years, this historic monument to popular French cooking continues to delight nostalgic customers with its old-fashioned, typically French atmosphere. In this quaint decor, where regulars used to keep their own napkin-rings in the buffet drawers, today's hungry locals and tourists searching for picture-postcard Paris come to eat classic French dishes: creamy egg mayonnaise, juicy steak and chips and the divine house-made whipped cream. Waiters and waitresses wearing black waistcoats and white aprons take orders directly on the table, where they also tot up the modest bill.

After twenty months spent in Los Angeles for the shoot of *Alien: Resurrection*, Jean-Pierre Jeunet enjoyed filming a Parisian night in the legendary and unchanging setting of this popular brasserie.

LE BOUILLON
CHARTIER
-
7, rue du Fg-Montmartre
75009 Paris
-
Ⓜ Grands-Boulevards
-
☎ 01 47 70 86 29
www.bouillon-chartier.com
-
Price:
★☆☆☆☆

WATCH THE TRAILER

ATHÉNÉE THÉÂTRE LOUIS-JOUVET

location for:

HUGO

by MARTIN SCORSESE

with ASA BUTTERFIELD, BEN KINGSLEY, SACHA BARON COHEN, CHLOE MORETZ

• 2011 •

Georges Méliès' magic tricks

ATHÉNÉE THÉÂTRE LOUIS-JOUVET
-
Square de l'Opéra-Louis-Jouvet
7, rue Boudreau
75009 Paris
-
Ⓜ Opéra
-
☎ 01 53 05 19 19
www.athenee-theatre.com
-
Price:
★★★☆☆

WATCH THE TRAILER

See also:
la bibliothèque Ste-Geneviève

The Athénée, formerly the Éden-Théâtre, was managed from 1934 until 1951 by the great actor Louis Jouvet, who gave it its identity as an advocate of contemporary theatre by offering audiences the rediscovery of great classics from Molière to Corneille and plays by Jean Giraudoux. His indelible influence forged the DNA of the theatre, which was renamed the Athénée Louis-Jouvet after his death. Pierre Bergé, the owner in 1977, brought Jean Marais, Delphine Seyrig and Sami Frey to public attention. He also created *Lundis musicaux* (musical Mondays), where the finest voices, including those of Barbara Hendricks, Ruggero Raimondi and Jessye Norman, were heard. In 1982, Pierre Bergé offered, for the nominal sum of one franc, to transfer administrative supervision to the French State, which accepted by making it a public theatre. This splendid Italian-style theatre, with perfect acoustics, today stages daring new productions of great dramatic works and opens its operas up to a wide audience under the direction of Patrice Martinet.

The 1930s setting of the Athénée, perfect for the film, fascinated Martin Scorsese, who came here several times when looking for a location for the magic scene.

SENDERENS

location for:

HEREAFTER

by CLINT EASTWOOD

with MATT DAMON, CÉCILE DE FRANCE, THIERRY NEUVIC

• 2011 •

Cécile de France and Thierry Neuvic discuss the meaning of life

SENDERENS
-
9, place de la Madeleine
75008 Paris

Ⓜ Madeleine

☎ 01 42 65 22 90
www.senderens.fr
-
Price:
★★★★☆

WATCH THE TRAILER

The year 1900 saw the opening of an English tavern with a sumptuous decor created by Majorelle, whose workers carved the woodwork from Ceylonese sycamore and lemon trees. Francis Carton bought it in 1925, transformed it into the Lucas Carton and steered it to three Michelin stars. Many top chefs were trained here under Chef Soustelle, among them Alain Senderens. On the strength of this early training, the latter then opened a restaurant, the Archestrate, which quickly rose to the ranks of three stars, but, nostalgic for his first restaurant, he eventually came back and acquired Lucas Carton in 1985. Against all odds and defying tradition, he surprised everyone in 2005 by giving up his very restrictive three stars, but not his apron: he renamed it Senderens and presented customers with a contemporary, seasonal menu at a quarter of the bill, with the same attention to subtle wine pairing suggestions, thus remaining faithful to his distinguished reputation.

Clint Eastwood, who had heard about Senderens, took advantage of long days on set to enjoy the wonderful langoustines, which are always on the menu.

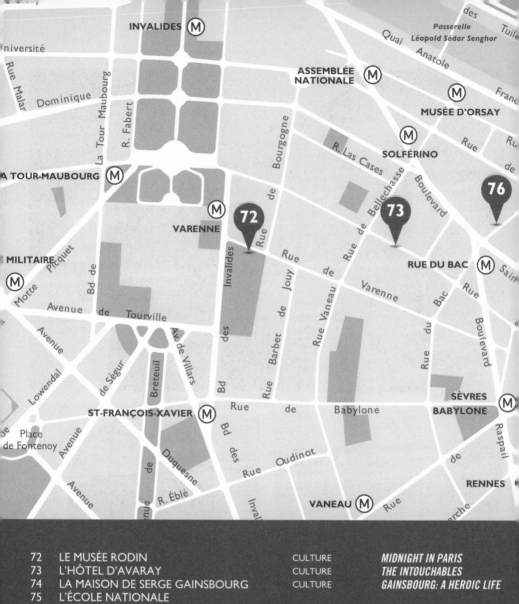

72	LE MUSÉE RODIN	CULTURE	*MIDNIGHT IN PARIS*
73	L'HÔTEL D'AVARAY	CULTURE	*THE INTOUCHABLES*
74	LA MAISON DE SERGE GAINSBOURG	CULTURE	*GAINSBOURG: A HEROIC LIFE*
75	L'ÉCOLE NATIONALE SUPÉRIEURE DES BEAUX-ARTS	CULTURE	*GAINSBOURG: A HEROIC LIFE*
76	DEYROLLE	SHOP	*MIDNIGHT IN PARIS*
77	LES DEUX MAGOTS	BRASSERIE	*THE INTOUCHABLES*
78	LE CAFÉ DE FLORE	BRASSERIE	*LOVE LASTS THREE YEARS*
79	LIPP	BRASSERIE	*TANGUY*
80	LE CAFÉ DE LA MAIRIE	BISTRO	*THE DISCREET*
81	L'ÉGLISE SAINT-SULPICE	CULTURE	*THE DA VINCI CODE*

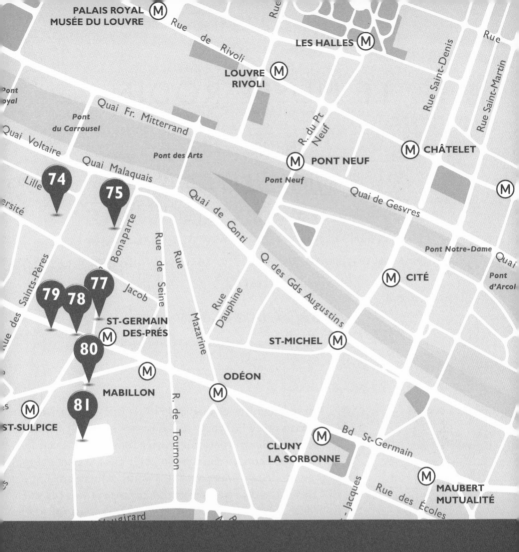

SAINT-GERMAIN
INVALIDES

LE MUSÉE RODIN

location for:

MIDNIGHT IN PARIS

by WOODY ALLEN

with OWEN WILSON, RACHEL MCADAMS, MICHAEL SHEEN,

MARION COTILLARD, KATHY BATES, CARLA BRUNI-SARKOZY

• 2011 •

Michael Sheen casts doubt on
Carla Bruni-Sarkozy's assertions about Camille

LE MUSÉE RODIN

-
79, rue de Varenne
75007 Paris
-
Ⓜ Varenne
-
☎ 01 44 18 61 10
www.musee-rodin.fr
-
Price:
★☆☆☆☆

WATCH THE TRAILER

See also:
le Bristol, Paul, Deyrolle,
Saint-Étienne-du-Mont, Polidor,
Shakespeare and Company

The museum was opened in 1919 on Rodin's initiative after he bequeathed his works to the French state. It is housed in the Hôtel Biron where the master remained a tenant until his death. Entirely renovated in 2012, this architectural gem presents on two floors the finest works of Rodin and Camille Claudel, as well as pieces from the sculptor's private collection. Hidden behind the building is the museum's pride and joy: its garden, a three-hectare haven of peace in the heart of Paris centering around an incredible rose garden and a magnificent parterre. Two thematic walks, the Jardin d'Orphée and the Jardin des Sources, have been created to help provide an understanding of the garden's layout. But whether you choose to follow a guide or prefer to stroll around on your own, it's impossible to miss *The Thinker*, *The Gates of Hell* and *The Burghers of Calais*, which stand in this green paradise. Rodin's kingdom also included a chapel that has been converted into the entrance foyer, a museum shop and an exhibition gallery. Woody Allen could not have found a better way to illustrate his hero's fanciful Parisian escape than to link him with Rodin's love life via *The Thinker*.

CULTURE

L'HÔTEL D'AVARAY

location for:

THE INTOUCHABLES

by ÉRIC TOLEDANO ET OLIVIER NAKACHE

with FRANÇOIS CLUZET, OMAR SY, ANNE LE NY, AUDREY FLEUROT

• 2011 •

François Cluzet's mansion

HÔTEL D'AVARAY
-
85, rue de Grenelle
75007 Paris
-
Ⓜ Solférino
-
www.amb-pays-bas.fr

*Open to the public only on
European Heritage Days*

WATCH THE TRAILER

See also:
le Nemours,
les Deux Magots,
la buvette des Marionnettes

The former home of the Bésiade d'Avaray family, the Hotel d'Avaray became the French residence of the Dutch Embassy in 1920. Located near the Ministry of Foreign Affairs with which it works closely, this diplomatic office organizes Franco-Dutch meetings via seminars, high-level talks and interviews with the Cooperation Council to strengthen relations between the two countries in order to develop, in particular, exchange opportunities in the fields of research and new technologies. The original Hotel Pozzo di Borgo being unavailable for filming, the Hotel Avaray very exceptionally agreed to host the film for two weeks during a diplomatic lull. At the ambassador's request, the entire fee was paid to the Cité Internationale Universitaire de Paris for the restoration of the Collège Néerlandais. Given the serious vocation of this diplomatic building, it is accessible to visitors only on European Heritage Days (*Journées du patrimoine*), when the Hotel d'Avaray opens its ground floor and garden to those in the know.

LA MAISON DE SERGE GAINSBOURG

location for:

GAINSBOURG: A HEROIC LIFE

by JOANN SFAR

with ÉRIC ELMOSNINO, LUCY GORDON, LÆTITIA CASTA,

DOUG JONES, ANNA MOUGLALIS, MYLÈNE JAMPANOÏ

• 2010 •

Devastated by their breakup, Serge Gainsbourg spends New Year's Eve alone in front of Bardot's portrait

LA MAISON DE
SERGE
GAINSBOURG
-
5 *bis*, rue de Verneuil
75006 Paris
-
Ⓜ Rue-du-Bac
-
Price:
☆☆☆☆☆

WATCH THE TRAILER

See also:
École nationale supérieure
des beaux-arts, Lapérouse

Tired of hiding his love for the married BB, in 1969 Serge Gainsbourg began looking for a discreet love nest for their illegitimate affair. On the advice of his father, he visited an old shop on the rue de Verneuil. He spent the last twenty years of his life in this classy duplex, which was renovated and painted black by interior decorator Andrée Higgins. The 'hôtel particulier', as he nicknamed it, is still not open to visitors, but its graffitied walls have elevated this legendary address to the status of a shrine, where tributes remain within easy reach of a good marker.

L'ÉCOLE NATIONALE SUPÉRIEURE DES BEAUX-ARTS

location for:

GAINSBOURG: A HEROIC LIFE

by JOANN SFAR

with ÉRIC ELMOSNINO, LUCY GORDON, LÆTITIA CASTA,

DOUG JONES, ANNA MOUGLALIS, MYLÈNE JAMPANOÏ

• 2010 •

Éric Elmosnino paints in the early morning

Created around the four fine arts – painting, sculpture, engraving and architecture – the school has been devoted exclusively to the visual arts since 1968. Its renowned teachers, studio-based training and privileged location in the midst of Paris's museums and their temporary exhibitions have made ENSBA famous worldwide. The sculptor César and the illustrator and director Joann Sfar both trained at this prestigious school. The latter set up his cameras in the morphology auditorium.

L'ÉCOLE NATIONALE
SUPÉRIEURE
DES BEAUX-ARTS
-
14, rue Bonaparte
75006 Paris
-
Ⓜ Saint-Germain-des-Prés
-
☎ 01 47 03 50 00
www.ensba.fr
-
Price:
☆☆☆☆☆
WATCH THE TRAILER

See also:
la maison de S. Gainsbourg,
Lapérouse

DEYROLLE

location for:

MIDNIGHT IN PARIS

by WOODY ALLEN

with OWEN WILSON, RACHEL MCADAMS, MICHAEL SHEEN, MARION COTILLARD,

KATHY BATES, CARLA BRUNI-SARKOZY

• 2011 •

Owen Wilson finds Marion Cotillard at a wedding reception

DEYROLLE
-
46, rue du Bac
75007 Paris
-
Ⓜ Rue-du-Bac
-
☎ 01 42 22 30 07
www.deyrolle.com
-
Price:
★★☆☆☆
WATCH THE TRAILER

See also: le Bristol,
le musée Rodin, Polidor,
Paul, Saint-Étienne-du-Mont,
Shakespeare and Company

Established in 1831, Deyrolle looks as though it has come straight out of Tim Burton's imagination. Along with its scientific materials, in France, one first encounters Deyrolle's pedagogical vocation via the famous colour illustrations of anatomy that adorn our classroom walls. But the taxidermy sector of its business is much more fascinating. On the first floor, a majestic giraffe in mid-stride welcomes you to a captivating, silent menagerie: a stationary lion, a placid elephant, a bewitching tiger, a menacing grizzly, a picturesque zebra and a wary baboon all await the adventurer ready to explore their eternal life. In this splendid mansion, you will also come across, mounted in the various showcases, tarantulas and poised butterflies and, on perches, multi-coloured birds surrounded by fossils. Rising from the ashes after a devastating fire in 2008, Deyrolle is now, like its immortal animals, enjoying a second magnificent life thanks to a fundraising initiative to help in its reconstruction.

This fantastical setting has inspired many directors, including Woody Allen for *Midnight in Paris* and Philippe Muyl for *Papillon*.

LES DEUX MAGOTS

location for:

THE INTOUCHABLES

by ÉRIC TOLEDANO ET OLIVIER NAKACHE

with FRANÇOIS CLUZET, OMAR SY, ANNE LE NY, AUDREY FLEUROT

· 2011 ·

An emotional meeting between Omar Sy and François Cluzet

LES DEUX MAGOTS
-
6, place St-Germain-des-Prés
75006 Paris
-
Ⓜ Saint-Germain-des-Prés
-
☎ 01 45 48 55 25
www.lesdeuxmagots.fr

Price:
★★★☆☆
WATCH THE TRAILER

See also:
le Nemours,
l'hôtel d'Avaray,
la buvette des Marionnettes

Les Deux Magots takes its name from a shop established in 1812 that itself was named after a play, *Les Deux Magots de Chine*. In 1885, the place became a *café-liquoriste* where Rimbaud, Verlaine and Mallarmé regularly met. In the 1920s it hosted the surrealists, led by André Breton, who were responsible for the creation of the Deux Magots literary prize, founded in 1933 to oppose the Goncourt Prize that had been awarded to Malraux for *La Condition Humaine* (Man's Fate), which they considered too academic. Its clientele then included many literary and artistic figures, including Picasso, Fernand Léger and Sartre, and today the worlds of fashion and politics rub shoulders here. The café menu offers classic salads, sandwiches and croques (toasted sandwiches), while the restaurant features seasonal French fare. Finally, the uniformed serving staff recommend that true gourmands try their famous old-fashioned hot chocolate, in which squares of chocolate are melted in milk.

The directors took over Les Deux Magots for an entire night to shoot numerous takes of this film, so many that Omar Sy nearly overdosed on chicken.

LE CAFÉ DE FLORE

location for:

LOVE LASTS THREE YEARS

by FRÉDÉRIC BEIGBEDER

with LOUISE BOURGOIN, GASPARD PROUST, JOEYSTARR,

JONATHAN LAMBERT, FRÉDÉRIQUE BEL, NICOLAS BEDOS

• 2012 •

Valérie Lemercier ends Gaspard Proust's anonymity

LE CAFÉ DE FLORE
-
172, bd Saint-Germain
75006 Paris
-
Ⓜ Saint-Germain-des-Prés
-
☎ 01 45 48 55 26
www.cafedeflore.fr
-
Price:
★★☆☆☆

See also:
le restaurant Amour

The Café de Flore is much more than just a café or restaurant. It's an institution, the pride and joy of the Left Bank. At the heart of the Quartier Saint-Germain since 1885, it takes its name from a sculpture of Flora, goddess of spring, which stands across the street. Frequented by Apollinaire with the young Breton and Aragon in the early the twentieth century, the Café de Flore became the meeting place of the literary world of Paris in the 1930s. But it was not until 1939, under its new owner, M. Boubal, that the already famous address became legendary. Among the Parisian intelligentsia who were drawn here were Sartre and Beauvoir, for whom the restaurant became a home away from home. Since being sold to M. Siljegovic in 1984, the Café de Flore has lost none of its charm. It continues to discreetly attract the intellectual and artistic elite along with loyal regulars whom the irreproachable waiters address by name, who come to enjoy a Club Rykiel with a glass of Ladoucette.

Frédéric Beigbeder is a regular at the Café de Flore and also founded the literary prize, the Prix de Flore, in 1994. Naturally, he paid tribute to the café in his film based on his novel of the same title.

LIPP

location for:

TANGUY

by ÉTIENNE CHATILIEZ

with ÉRIC BERGER, SABINE AZÉMA, ANDRÉ DUSSOLLIER, HÉLÈNE DUC,

AURORE CLÉMENT, JEAN-PAUL ROUVE, ANDRÉ WILMS

• 2001 •

Philippe Gildas interrupts yet another dispute about 'the Pekingese'

LIPP
-
151, bd Saint-Germain
75006 Paris
-
Ⓜ Saint-Germain-des-Prés
-
☎ 01 45 48 53 91
www.groupe-bertrand.com
/lipp.php
-
Price:
★★☆☆☆

WATCH THE TRAILER

When they opened the brasserie in 1880, Léonard Lipp and his wife Pétronille never imagined that a restaurant serving sauerkraut washed down with beer would soon become so popular with Parisian high society. Forty years later, Marcellin Cazes bought the place, which was already being patronized by Verlaine and Apollinaire, and later created the Cazes Prize, which is awarded to a writer who has never won any other literary prize. Over the years, the Brasserie Lipp has become popular with the cultural and political elite of Paris. Incidentally, fate would have it that the affair of Ben Barka, who politically opposed Morocco's King Hassan II, would begin with his abduction in front of the restaurant. Today a flagship of the Groupe Bertrand, the institution has retained its charm and splendour with its varnished mahogany façade and its ceramic murals by Léon Fargues. The menu, meanwhile, keeps tradition alive, giving pride of place to dishes such as leeks vinaigrette and rum baba, which are served by waiters with white napkins at the ready.

Used by Francis Girod for a few shots in *Le Bon Plaisir*, Lipp is primarily a place for family meetings in Étienne Chatiliez's *Tanguy*.

.

.

LE CAFÉ DE LA MAIRIE

location for:

THE DISCREET

by CHRISTIAN VINCENT

with FABRICE LUCHINI, MAURICE GARREL, JUDITH HENRY, MARIE BUNEL, FRANÇOIS TOUMARKINE, BRICE BEAUGIER, SERGE RIABOUKINE

• 1990 •

Fabrice Luchini waits for Judith Henri at the Café de la Mairie

LE CAFÉ
DE LA MAIRIE
-
8, place Saint-Sulpice
75006 Paris
-
Ⓜ Saint-Sulpice
-
☎ 01 43 26 67 82
-
Price:
★☆☆☆☆

WATCH THE TRAILER

Especially sought after on fine days for its large terrace ideally situated on the Place Saint-Sulpice, the Café de la Mairie has all the glitz of a popular neighbourhood bistro. Intellectuals, artists and pretty young women exhausted at the end of an afternoon's shopping come here to enjoy a quiet moment, the only sound being the bells from the neighbouring parish. The simple menu doesn't detract from the place's Parisian charm. It's hardly surprising that Fabrice Luchini was a regular here in *The Discreet*.

L'ÉGLISE SAINT-SULPICE

location for:

THE DA VINCI CODE

by RON HOWARD

with TOM HANKS, AUDREY TAUTOU, JEAN RENO, IAN MCKELLEN,

ALFRED MOLINA, PAUL BETTANY, JEAN-PIERRE MARIELLE

• 2006 •

Paul Bettany comes to search for the keystone

The church of Saint-Sulpice is dedicated to Sulpitius the Pious, the Bishop of Bourges in the seventh century. Its construction from 1660 to 1870 explains its unique style. Visits of the interior are made in silence out of respect for worshippers for, in addition to religious services, the Chapel of the Virgin, the pulpit of the central nave and the frescos by Delacroix also offer an incredible wealth of art. In order to accommodate the totally fictitious 'history' behind the plot of *The Da Vinci Code*, the interior of Saint-Sulpice was completely replicated in a studio.

L'ÉGLISE
SAINT-SULPICE
-
50, rue de Vaugirard
75006 Paris
-
Ⓜ Saint-Sulpice
-
☎ 01 42 34 59 98
www.paroisse-saint-sulpice-
paris.org

WATCH THE TRAILER

82	LA BUVETTE DES MARIONNETTES	BAR	THE INTOUCHABLES
83	POLIDOR	RESTAURANT	MIDNIGHT IN PARIS
84	ESPACE ACCATTONE	CULTURE	2 DAYS IN PARIS
85	DUBOIS	SHOP	CONVERSATIONS WITH MY GARDENER
86	LE MARCHÉ MAUBERT	SHOP	CHANGE OF PLANS
87	SAINT-ÉTIENNE-DU-MONT	CULTURE	MIDNIGHT IN PARIS
88	LA BIBLIOTHÈQUE SAINTE-GENEVIÈVE	CULTURE	HUGO
89	THE BOMBARDIER	PUB	'LOLITA' – THE PLAYERŚ
90	LE PIANO VACHE	BAR	GOOD OLD DAZE
91	LA PISCINE MUNICIPALE PONTOISE	EXPERIENCE	THREE COLOURS: BLUE
92	SHAKESPEARE AND COMPANY	SHOP	BEFORE SUNSET
93	LE CAVEAU DE LA HUCHETTE	CLUB	HAPPINESS NEVER COMES ALONE
94	LAPÉROUSE	RESTAURANT	GAINSBOURG: A HEROIC LIFE

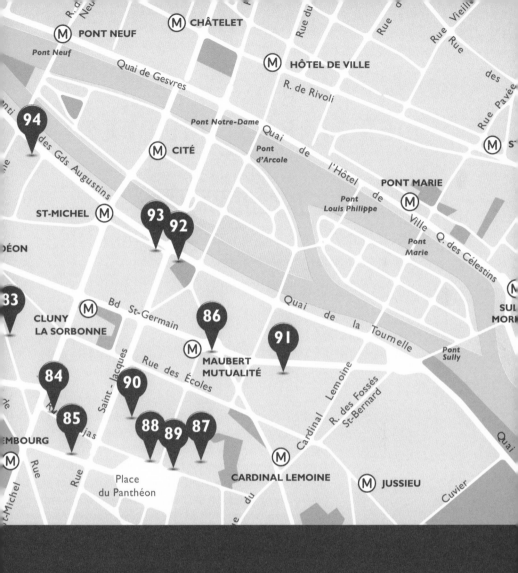

M PONT NEUF
Pont Neuf
M CHÂTELET
Quai de Gesvres
M HÔTEL DE VILLE
R. de Rivoli
Rue du
Rue
Rue Vieille
Rue
des
Rue Pavée
94
des Gds Augustins
Pont Notre-Dame
M CITÉ
Quai de l'Hôtel
Pont d'Arcole
M S
PONT MARIE
Pont Louis Philippe
M
Ville
Q. des Célestins
Pont Marie
ST-MICHEL M
93 92
ÉON
33
CLUNY
LA SORBONNE
M
Bd St-Germain
Quai de la Tournelle
Pont Sully
SUL
MOR
M
86
91
Saint-Jacques
Rue des Écoles
M
MAUBERT
MUTUALITÉ
Cardinal Lemoine
R. des Fossés St-Bernard
Quai
84
90
MBOURG
M
85
jas
Rue
Rue
88 89 87
Place
du Panthéon
M
CARDINAL LEMOINE
du
M JUSSIEU
Cuvier

QUARTIER LATIN

LA BUVETTE DES MARIONNETTES

location for:

THE INTOUCHABLES

by ÉRIC TOLEDANO AND OLIVIER NAKACHE

with FRANÇOIS CLUZET, OMAR SY, ANNE LE NY, AUDREY FLEUROT

• 2011 •

Grégoire Oestermann advises François Cluzet to be wary of Omar Sy

LA BUVETTE DES MARIONNETTES
-
Jardin du Luxembourg
75006 Paris
-
Ⓜ Luxembourg
-
☎ 01 43 26 33 04
www.senat.fr
-
Price:
★☆☆☆☆
WATCH THE TRAILER

See also:
l'hôtel d'Avaray, le Nemours,
les Deux Magots

Tucked away in the Jardin du Luxembourg, near the children's playground and the puppet theatre, the Buvette des Marionnettes offers a chance to stop and have something tasty to eat after a pleasant walk along the paths bordering the Senate. A truly bucolic experience, you'll feel as though you're having a break in the country as you sit down with your family to sip a cold drink on the shaded terrace or fill up on a Guignol panini to the delight of children who've been playing in the garden. You may find yourselves sitting beside exhausted tennis players who've come for some refreshment before finishing their match on the courts next to the park. Although the place is usually crowded in the summer, it's much easier to find a table in the winter, when you can warm up with a cappuccino while you admire the statues lining the paths. If you're sensitive to the cold, there are a few tables inside, where you can savour the house special, a hot toasted Poilâne sandwich, or devour a caramel and salted butter crêpe.

The directors of *The Intouchables* had no problem taking over the place because it was snowing heavily on the day of the shoot and the park was closed to the public.

POLIDOR

location for:

MIDNIGHT IN PARIS

by WOODY ALLEN

with OWEN WILSON, RACHEL MCADAMS, MICHAEL SHEEN,

MARION COTILLARD, KATHY BATES, CARLA BRUNI-SARKOZY

• 2011 •

Owen Wilson meets Ernest Hemingway

POLIDOR
-
41, rue Monsieur-le-Prince
75006 Paris
-
Ⓜ Odéon
-
☎ 01 43 26 95 34
www.polidor.com
-
Price:
★★☆☆☆

WATCH THE TRAILER

See also:
Paul, le musée Rodin, Deyrolle,
Shakespeare and Company,
Saint-Étienne-du-Mont

A true institution a stone's throw from the Odéon, Polidor is picture-postcard Paris. Its frontage is its best publicity: the one hundred and fifty year-old restaurant hasn't changed since the beginning of the last century. Seating is at large tables where everyone mixes with their neighbours. The first room is decorated in a miscellany of styles with old furniture and a few amateur paintings, a sketch by Pierre Dac, *La Recette de la sauce aux câpres sans câpres* (*The Recipe for Caper Sauce Without Capers*), and cooking diplomas displayed on the walls. For purists, the room at the back hosted, until 1975, the College of 'Pataphysics, whose guests included René Clair, Boris Vian, Ionesco and Paul Émile Victor. The place continues to attract generations of writers, painters and researchers as well as families, offering traditional dishes in authentic, quaint surroundings: after a classic egg mayonnaise and a not-to-be-missed *petit salé aux lentilles* (salted lean pork belly with lentils), everyone will love the tarte Tatin.

Woody Allen successfully staged his hero's journey through time in this restaurant's dated atmosphere. Be warned: perhaps nostalgic for another era, Polidor accepts only cash.

Victor Hugo, Ernest Hemingway, Paul Verlaine and Arthur Rimbaud were regulars at Polidor

*A programme with
no inhibitions or taboos*

ESPACE ACCATTONE

location for:

2 DAYS IN PARIS

by JULIE DELPY

with JULIE DELPY, ADAM GOLDBERG, MARIE PILLET,

ALBERT DELPY, ALEXIA LANDEAU, ALEXANDRE NAHON

• 2007 •

Julie Delpy takes Adam Goldberg to a provocative photo exhibit

This former Gipsy cabaret where Edith Piaf performed was transformed, in 1957, into a cinema, the Studio Cujas, which initially focused on American films before redirecting its attention to French arthouse films. It was not until thirty years later that Kazik Hentchel, a Polish writer and art lover, bought the cinema and renamed it the Accattone after the title of Pier Paolo Pasolini's first film.

The single auditorium was then refurbished and modernized and programming has since focused exclusively on auteur films. Informed film lovers can see around thirty previously unreleased, cutting edge films a week, with a different film at each screening. In addition, the Accattone opens out onto a mixed-use space with a bar, a bookstall offering the works adapted for the screen and a gallery displaying photographs from the world of the films being screened.

It was not by chance that Julie Delpy set up her cameras at this unique place to shoot the gallery opening. In fact, she knows the Accattone well through her parents: they come here regularly and her father has exhibited here.

ESPACE
ACCATTONE
-
20, rue Cujas
75005 Paris
-
Ⓜ Cluny-La-Sorbonne

☎ 01 46 33 86 86
-
Price:
★☆☆☆☆

WATCH THE TRAILER

DUBOIS

location for:

CONVERSATIONS WITH MY GARDENER

by JEAN BECKER

with DANIEL AUTEUIL, JEAN-PIERRE DARROUSSIN, FANNY COTTENÇON

• 2007 •

Daniel Auteuil has come to restock his painting materials

DUBOIS

-

20, rue Soufflot
75005 Paris

-

Ⓜ Luxembourg

-

☎ 01 44 41 67 50
www.dubois-paris.com

-

Price:
★★☆☆☆

See also:
le Nemours

Founded in 1861, Dubois was originally a manufacturer of extra-fine Merlin Denis colours. Over the centuries, it has established itself as the Parisian benchmark for art lovers, while remaining a family-run company.

From extra-fine oil paints to the gouaches we used as children, from short-handled brushes for watercolours to long-handled ones for painting with oils and synthetic ones for acrylics, via canvas sold by the metre or mounted and framed, without forgetting the modeling clay, the shop's two floors display an unrivaled palette of materials. All brands, even the oldest ones, are available, along with advice from informed and passionate experts. Every month, trends are celebrated with a pick of favourite new products. Finally, the shop stays humble by not overlooking the first steps, offering beginners a discerning selection of instructional books and videos aimed at helping them discover, learn and improve their skills.

Jean Becker naturally chose this setting to establish his hero as a well-known Parisian painter, allowing him to evolve as a regular customer of the shop.

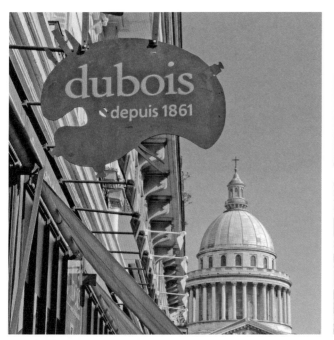

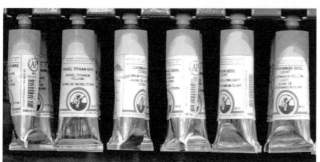

LE MARCHÉ MAUBERT

location for:

CHANGE OF PLANS

by DANIÈLE THOMPSON

with KARIN VIARD, DANY BOON, MARINA FOÏS, PATRICK BRUEL, MARINA HANDS,

EMMANUELLE SEIGNER, CHRISTOPHER THOMPSON, PATRICK CHESNAIS

• 2009 •

Karin Viard shops for dinner

LE MARCHÉ MAUBERT
-
Place Maubert
75005 Paris
-
Ⓜ Maubert-Mutualité
-
Hours:
Tuesday and Thursday
7am–2.30pm,
Saturday 7am–3pm
-
Price:
★★☆☆☆
WATCH THE TRAILER

See also:
les Ombres, le Pure Café,
le Zéphyr, Point Éphémère,
la Halle aux Oliviers

Maubert Market, one of the oldest in Paris, is famous for its market gardeners and florists. It feels like being in the country. After a joyful stroll between the stalls to gather a basketful of fresh, local produce, we linger in front of the clothes stalls, dither in front of the litany of useful and useless objects that have caught our eye and always end up wandering around the nearby shops to track down organic goodies.

Maubert being also renowned for its exceptional cheeses, Danièle Thompson filmed Karin Viard in front of a cheese stall.

SAINT-ÉTIENNE-DU-MONT

location for:

MIDNIGHT IN PARIS

by WOODY ALLEN

with OWEN WILSON, RACHEL MCADAMS, MICHAEL SHEEN,

MARION COTILLARD, KATHY BATES, CARLA BRUNI-SARKOZY

• 2011 •

Owen Wilson's midnight rendez-vous in Paris

The church of Saint-Étienne-Du-Mont, classified as an historic monument, displays a combination of Gothic and Renaissance architecture. The first thing that strikes you is the unusual façade, then the amazing choir screen inside. A complete set of stained glass windows and the organ case, the oldest in Paris, complete the visit. Pascal, Racine and Sainte Geneviève, the patron saint of Paris, are buried here, and John Paul II celebrated a mass here in 1997. You won't need to wait for the stroke of midnight to lose yourself in this romantic interior.

SAINT-ÉTIENNE
DU-MONT
-
Place Sainte-Geneviève
75005 Paris
-
Ⓜ Maubert-Mutualité
or Cardinal-Lemoine
-
☎ 01 43 54 11 79
www.saintetiennedumont.fr

WATCH THE TRAILER

See also:
Paul, le musée Rodin,
le Bristol, Deyrolle, Polidor,
Shakespeare and Company

LA BIBLIOTHÈQUE SAINTE-GENEVIÈVE

location for:

HUGO

by MARTIN SCORSESE

with ASA BUTTERFIELD, BEN KINGSLEY,

SACHA BARON COHEN, CHLOE MORETZ

• 2011 •

Hugo and Isabelle discover the history of the cinema

LA BIBLIOTHÈQUE
SAINTE-GENEVIÈVE
-
10, place du Panthéon
75005 Paris
-
Ⓜ Luxembourg
or Maubert-Mutualité
-
☎ 01 44 41 97 97
www-bsg.univ-paris1.fr
-
Price:
☆☆☆☆☆
WATCH THE TRAILER

See also:
Athénée théâtre Louis-Jouvet

The Sainte-Geneviève Library is named after one of the oldest Parisian abbeys, which dates from the sixth century and now houses the Lycée Henri IV. Rebuilt in 1851 on the site of the former Collège de Montaigu, then expanded and classified as a historical monument, it has retained its magnificent fixtures and its original interior. Today, it is the third oldest library in Europe. Both an inter-varsity and a public library, it is open to all adults, holders of the baccalaureate and even simply curious visitors accompanied by a guide (usually a student). Its collection of works totals nearly two million volumes and is consulted by seven hundred students daily. The huge reading room, where the only distractions are the books and the bluish light from the lamps, provides a setting conducive to silent concentration.

Although most of the film sets were easy to take from those of the illustrated book by Brian Selznick, Scorsese needed to find a library that embodied the author's overflowing imagination. The Sainte-Geneviève Library brought the end of the story to life.

THE BOMBARDIER

location for:

'LOLITA' – THE PLAYERS

by ÉRIC LARTIGAU

with GILLES LELLOUCHE, JEAN DUJARDIN

• 2012 •

Gilles Lellouche finds his 'Lolita' surrounded by her friends

THE BOMBARDIER
-
2, place du Panthéon
75005 Paris
-
Ⓜ Maubert-Mutualité
or Cardinal-Lemoine
-
☎ 01 43 54 79 22
www.bombardierpub.fr

Price:
★☆☆☆☆

WATCH THE TRAILER

See also:
Point Éphémère,
le Pure Café

The Bombardier is an English pub that's so authentic you'll as though you're in the heart of London: wood panelling, wooden ceiling beams, stained glass windows, slates displaying sporting-calendar events, old carpet and service at the bar by a certified 100% British staff. The atmosphere is relaxed and entertainment is provided by darts matches and pub quizzes on Sunday nights; the immersion into British culture is complete when there's football or rugby on the television: Brits then take over the pub and the place buzzes with the action of the match. A non-stop round of pints begins, the draught beer imported directly from the Wells and Young's brewery in Bedfordshire to the great delight of beer drinkers. For a truly British culinary experience, classic fish 'n' chips and the traditional curry are prepared every lunchtime, full English breakfast is available at weekends and a famous roast dinner is served on Sundays.

Lartigau filmed Gilles Lellouche surrounded by students in this pub, which attracts a local university crowd with its friendly atmosphere and a happy hour that lasts from 5pm to 9pm daily.

LE PIANO VACHE

location for:

GOOD OLD DAZE

by CÉDRIC KLAPISCH

with ROMAIN DURIS, VINCENT ELBAZ, NICOLAS KORETZKY,

JULIEN LAMBROSCHINI, JOACHIM LOMBARD

• 1995 •

*Jackie Berroyer sings the praises
of Kathmandu to Romain Duris and Julien Lambroschini*

Le Piano Vache has held on to its teen-rebel soul and rock attitude since 1969. Its subdued lighting and shabby decor, old brick walls covered in graffiti and cult film and underground concert posters, transport customers straight back to an 'old school' atmosphere.

People come here in the evening with their mates to knock back a pint or two or drink cocktails and gyrate to the sounds blasted out by the evening's resident DJ: gothic, rock, '80s night or the famous Friday-night *Chewing-gum des oreilles* (Chewing gum for the ears), a fun mix of pop-rock from the 1960s to the present day guaranteed to energize your ears. At lunchtime on weekdays, it's a great place to grab a quick bite to eat: a panini, a salad, sausage and chips, or the amazing *croque-monsieur du Cap-Vert*.

Cédric Klapisch isn't the only one to have set up his cameras at Le Piano Vache: singer-actor Patrick Bruel also immortalized it by making it the meeting place ten years hence for his student friends in his music video 'Place des Grands-Hommes'.

LE PIANO VACHE
-
8, rue Laplace
75005 Paris
-
Ⓜ Maubert-Mutualité
-
☎ 01 46 33 75 03
www.lepianovache.com
-
Price:
★☆☆☆☆

WATCH THE TRAILER

*Become part
of the legend by
stapling your ID photo
to the wall*

LA PISCINE MUNICIPALE PONTOISE

location for:

THREE COLOURS: BLUE

by KRZYSZTOF KIEŚLOWSKI

with JULIETTE BINOCHE, CHARLOTTE VÉRY, BENOÎT RÉGENT

• 1993 •

Juliette Binoche's nighttime swims

LA PISCINE MUNICIPALE PONTOISE

-

19, rue de Pontoise
75005 Paris

-

Ⓜ Maubert-Mutualité

-

☎ 01 55 42 77 88
www.carilis.fr/francais/
espace-sportif-pontoise

-

Price:
★☆☆☆☆

WATCH THE TRAILER

Feel like diving headfirst into a blue sea? Welcome to Pontoise swimming pool, which will launch you into its retro atmosphere and immerse you in the crazy world of the 1930s. Its thirty-three-metre pool certainly appeals to swimmers, but the setting also takes your breath away: two floors of changing cubicles around a walkway and the glass roof give this place an allegorical charm. Behind the remarkable architecture, the sports complex has evolved to meet present-day expectations, with two saunas, a cardio room, bodybuilding equipment and four squash courts. The final touch: the swimming pool opens its doors to swimmers every weekday evening until midnight, with subdued lighting and background music. The establishment, built in 1934, is a classified historical monument.

Krzysztof Kieślowski couldn't but have Juliette Binoche swim here at nighttime in Three Colours: Blue. You'll also find Emmanuelle Béart floating in this setting in Nelly and M. Arnaud. Finally, Amélie's father is introduced to us at the beginning of the film getting out of this pool.

SHAKESPEARE AND COMPANY

location for:

BEFORE SUNSET

by RICHARD LINKLATER

with JULIE DELPY, ETHAN HAWKE

• 2005 •

Julie Delpy meets Ethan Hawke again several years after Before Sunrise

SHAKESPEARE
AND COMPANY
-
37, rue de la Bûcherie
75005 Paris
-
Ⓜ Saint-Michel
-
☎ 01 43 25 40 93
shakespeareandcompany.com
-
Price:
★★☆☆☆

WATCH THE TRAILER

See also:
le Pure Café

Bookstore or library, Shakespeare and Company is above all an institution specializing in literature in English since 1951. The shop has seen a stream of writers and customers, including Henry Miller, who called it the wonderland of books. It late owner George Whitman used to describe it as a socialist utopia pretending to be a bookshop. His daughter Sylvia has breathed new life into it since taking over in 2001, but the spirit of its founder lives on: rare books, classics and recent publications are still stacked up on shelves across two floors giving the place an appearance worthy of Hogwarts. The shop continues to host writers looking for a place to stay, on thirteen banquettes placed among the stacks, on condition that they help with sales for a minimum of two hours a day and read a book a day. Finally, it continues its mission to introduce people to books and authors with weekly readings and a yearly festival.

In addition to Before Sunset, Shakespeare and Company hosted the film crew of *Julie & Julia*, and Woody Allen, a loyal fan of this bookstore, filmed part of *Midnight in Paris* here.

CLUB

LE CAVEAU DE LA HUCHETTE

location for:

HAPPINESS NEVER COMES ALONE

by JAMES HUTH

with SOPHIE MARCEAU, GAD ELMALEH, FRANÇOIS BERLÉAND

• 2012 •

Gad Elmaleh on stage

LE CAVEAU
DE LA HUCHETTE
-
5, rue de la Huchette
75005 Paris
-
Ⓜ Saint-Michel
-
☎ 01 43 26 65 05
www.caveaudelahuchette.fr
-
Price:
★★☆☆☆

WATCH THE TRAILER

Long before its love affair with music, Caveau de la Huchette played an important role in French history. Originally a meeting place for the Templars in the sixteenth century, the two superimposed cellars and the upper room, serving as a tavern, were used during the Revolution as a tribunal, prison and execution room. The very deep well into which the bodies disappeared still exists in the lower cellar. In fact, everything remains intact, and if the weapons attached to the walls send shivers down your spine, the chastity belt will also cause a shudder. Much later, in 1946, the frenzy of the Liberation would dance to the sounds of swing brought by GIs into the cellars of the Left Bank, now transformed into dance floors. Caveau de la Huchette would become the first club in Paris to play jazz and has continued ever since to feature the greatest names, including Count Basie, Sidney Bechet, Memphis Slim, in an atmosphere that is still often compared to the heyday of the Cotton Club.

The cellar of Caveau de la Huchette was a natural choice for Gad Elmaleh playing a jazz pianist in the the film *Happiness Never Comes Alone*.

LAPÉROUSE

location for:

GAINSBOURG: A HEROIC LIFE

by JOANN SFAR

with ÉRIC ELMOSNINO, LUCY GORDON, LÆTITIA CASTA, DOUG JONES,

ANNA MOUGLALIS, MYLÈNE JAMPANOÏ

• 2010 •

Éric Elmosnino hasn't yet succumbed to Lucy Gordon's charms

LAPÉROUSE

-

51, quai des Grands-Augustins
75006 Paris

-

Ⓜ Pont-Neuf
or Saint-Michel

-

☎ 01 43 26 68 04
www.laperouse.fr

Price:
★★★☆☆

WATCH THE TRAILER

See also:
la maison de S. Gainsbourg,
l'École nationale supérieure
des beaux-arts

A former eighteenth-century mansion marked by two hundred and fifty years of history, Lapérouse is sought after for the intimate and sumptuous ambiance of its first-floor rooms, which were originally servants quarters, then transformed into accounting offices and subsequently used for romantic rendez-vous. One of the boudoirs, named the Victor Hugo, pays tribute to its most famous regular. Prized today by couples seeking a romantic setting, these rooms are also used for business lunches where privacy is of the essence. Its choice dishes, which remain true to traditional recipes, preserve the reputation of the establishment while being updated by Chef Christophe Guibert. A tradition of excellence is upheld by this restaurant, which is inscribed in the history of French gastronomy as one of the first restaurants to be awarded three Michelin stars in 1951.

Although the real meeting between Serge Gainsbourg and Jane Birkin, the 1970s most glamourous couple, didn't take place here, the director immortalised the moment chez Lapérouse because of its sumptuous and seductive decor.

95	LA COUPOLE	RESTAURANT	*HUNTING AND GATHERING*
96	LA CLOSERIE DES LILAS	RESTAURANT	*SAGAN*
97	LE VERRE À PIED	BAR	*AMÉLIE*
98	LE STUDIO DES URSULINES	CULTURE	*JULES AND JIM*
99	LES GRANDES SERRES		
	DU JARDIN DES PLANTES	EXPERIENCE	*A MONSTER IN PARIS*
100	LES CAILLOUX	RESTAURANT	*DELICACY*
101	LA CAVE LA BOURGOGNE	BISTRO	*MUNICH*

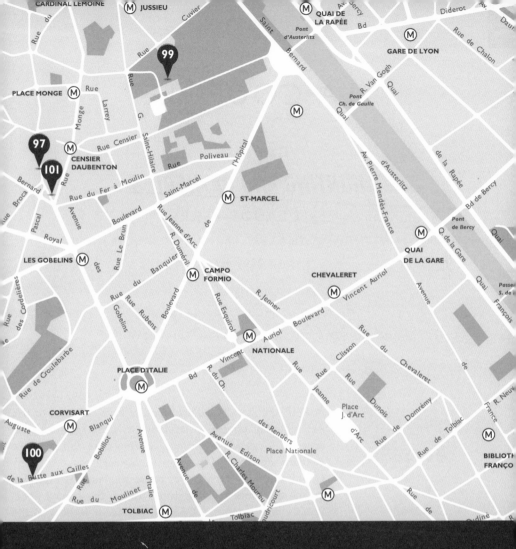

PORT-ROYAL
JARDIN DES PLANTES

LA COUPOLE

location for:

HUNTING AND GATHERING

by CLAUDE BERRI

with AUDREY TAUTOU, GUILLAUME CANET, LAURENT STOCKER, FRANÇOISE BERTIN

• 2007 •

*Audrey Tautou, Guillaume Canet
and Laurent Stocker celebrate New Year's Eve*

LA COUPOLE
-
102, bd du Montparnasse
75014 Paris
-
Ⓜ Vavin
-
☎ 01 43 20 14 20
www.lacoupole-paris.com
-
Price:
★★★☆☆

See also:
le Tokyo Eat

In 1927, the literary and art world of Paris hastened to this Art Nouveau temple to celebrate its opening in splendid style with a cascade of Champagne. They came to admire the columns and pilasters, the place's crowning glory, created by twenty-seven painters, and to praise the Pergola restaurant on the first floor and the dance hall on the ground floor. From that moment, La Coupole became a witness to the Paris of the Roaring Twenties, each table becoming part of its story: Camus celebrated his Nobel Prize at his usual table 149, Gainsbourg and Birkin regularly lunched at table 24, while Coluche met Véronique Kantor at table 128 and François Mitterrand ordered his last lamb curry, a house special since 1927, at table 82. Every day, tourists flock here to recapture the spirit of Hemingway in *A Moveable Feast*, the work that made this Parisian brasserie world famous.

The film world has naturally seized on this legendary place: in addition to Claude Berri's film, La Coupole can be seen in *La Boum*, where Poupette receives at her usual table her darling Vic, who's amazed by the brasserie's splendour.

LA CLOSERIE DES LILAS

location for:

SAGAN

by DIANE KURYS

with SYLVIE TESTUD, PIERRE PALMADE, JEANNE BALIBAR,

LIONEL ABELANSKI, ARIELLE DOMBASLE, DENIS PODALYDÈS

• 2008 •

Sylvie Testud meets Pierre Palmade for lunch

**LA CLOSERIE
DES LILAS**
-
171, bd du Montparnasse
75006 Paris
-
Ⓜ Raspail
or RER Port-Royal
-
☎ 01 40 51 34 50
www.closeriedeslilas.fr

Price:
★★★☆☆

WATCH THE TRAILER

Since the nineteenth century, La Closerie des Lilas has been a popular meeting place for artists. It started out as a coaching tavern before being transformed into an open-air café with a flower-covered arbour that, as soon as it opened, began to attract customers who had come to have a wild time at the neighbouring Bullier dance hall set up in a garden of lilac. Zola and the Goncourt brothers soon became regulars and the café rapidly became a hotspot of Parisian cultural nightlife. With patrons like Verlaine and Modigliani, its fame also crossed the Atlantic: American celebrities in Paris flocked here. Fitzgerald is rumored to have read the manuscript of *The Great Gatsby* to Hemingway at La Closerie. Today, the establishment includes a chic restaurant where you dine on a covered terrace and a more affordable brasserie, as well as a piano-bar decorated in warm wood, where a little silver plaque on the bar marks the spot where Ernest Hemingway regularly sat.

Sylvie Testud as Françoise Sagan was naturally filmed as a regular at La Closerie des Lilas in Diane Kurys' film, and Robert Enrico used the location to shoot Romy Schneider and Philippe Noiret's legendary dinner in *The Old Gun*.

LE VERRE À PIED

location for:

AMÉLIE

by JEAN-PIERRE JEUNET

with AUDREY TAUTOU, MATHIEU KASSOVITZ, ISABELLE NANTY

• 2001 •

Dominique Bretodeau regains his composure

LE VERRE À PIED
-
118 *bis*, rue Mouffetard
75005 Paris
-
Ⓜ Censier-Daubenton
-
☎ 01 43 31 15 72
www.leverreapied.fr

Price:
★☆☆☆☆

WATCH THE TRAILER

See also:
le café des 2 Moulins, Studio 28
au marché de la Butte

Le Verre à Pied has established itself as an invaluable, providential place to stop on the bustling rue Mouffetard. This old-fashioned bistro welcomes its customers unaffectedly with sincere smiles that are lit up by a timeless decor, which gives it a delightfully Bohemian ambiance. During the day, students, local shopkeepers, artists and retired teachers sit down to have a drink and talk, stimulated by the friendly atmosphere. Regulars also meet up for literary evenings or to view the latest exhibits displayed on the walls, which fuel fevered debates. Sightseers will find a typically French bistro with an antique cast-iron stove, quaint tiles and old burnished wooden chairs and tables, the perfect setting to enjoy homemade, traditional, well-priced food and an excellent glass of wine.

This charming, authentic place led Jean-Pierre Jeunet to abandon Montmartre for one scene in favour of the Left Bank. The director set up his cameras at Le Verre à Pied for two days to film a few unforgettable, emotional minutes.

LE STUDIO DES URSULINES

location for:

JULES AND JIM

by FRANÇOIS TRUFFAUT

with JEANNE MOREAU, OSKAR WERNER, HENRI SERRE, MARIE DUBOIS,

BORIS BASSIAK, VANNA URBINO, ANNIE NELSEN

• 1962 •

Jim meets up with Jules and Catherine at the cinema

**LE STUDIO
DES URSULINES**

-

10, rue des Ursulines
75005 Paris

-

Ⓜ Censier-Daubenton
or RER Luxembourg

-

☎ 01 56 81 15 20
www.studiodesursulines.com

Price:
★☆☆☆☆

WATCH THE TRAILER

Since its creation in 1925, the Studio des Ursulines has devoted itself to screening previously unreleased avant-garde films. It was the precursor of what, since 1955, have been called *salles art et essai* (arthouse cinemas). The studio, which has always remained independent, has never lost its mission of presenting films far removed from the world of blockbusters and, since 2003, has focused its attention specifically on young people, with a discerning choice of educational and cultural films. In tribute to this independent cinema, François Truffaut decided to shoot the cinema scene of *Jules and Jim* here.

LES GRANDES DU JARDIN DES PLANTES

Inspiration for:

A MONSTER IN PARIS

by ÉRIC BERGERON

with the voices of VANESSA PARADIS, M

• 2011 •

The birth of Francœur

Fancy a romantic stroll in a novel setting or a family outing with an educational bent? The big glasshouses of the Jardin des Plantes (botanical garden) offer a journey to the heart of luxuriant biodiversity on a fun but informative trail. For over three hundred years, these enormous glass-and-steel greenhouses, built to preserve and acclimatize plants from all over the world, have amassed a collection of the rarest and strangest botanical species for the discovery and wonder of all.

LES GRANDES
SERRES DU JARDIN
DES PLANTES

-

36, rue Geoffroy-St-Hilaire
75005 Paris

-

Ⓜ Censier-Daubenton

-

☎ 01 40 79 56 01
www.jardindesplantes.net

-

Price:
★☆☆☆☆

WATCH THE TRAILER

See also:
le funiculaire de Montmartre

LES CAILLOUX

location for:

DELICACY

by DAVID AND STÉPHANE FOENKINOS

with AUDREY TAUTOU, FRANÇOIS DAMIENS, BRUNO TODESCHINI,

PIO MARMAI, JOSÉPHINE DE MEAUX

• 2011 •

Pio Marmai succumbs to Audrey Tautou's charms

LES CAILLOUX

-

58, rue des Cinq-Diamants
75013 Paris

-

Ⓜ Corvisart

-

☎ 01 45 80 15 08

-

Price:
★★☆☆☆

WATCH THE TRAILER

Les Cailloux, at the top of the very pretty Butte aux Cailles, was the first restaurant Julien Cohen opened. With a terrace that's popular with neighbourhood regulars on sunny days, this charming restaurant leaves no one indifferent. Its elegant taupe façade and large windows invite you into a chic and understated interior, decorated in New York style with subdued lighting and an old, untreated parquet floor. There is no hint, apart from the waitresses' lilting accents, of the succulent Italian cuisine, Florentine in inspiration, that awaits. Along with the aubergine *millefeuille*, the *tagliata* of beef with artichokes, or the *terracotta* dessert upon which your tastebuds will feast, you will find equally exquisite and well-chosen wines. It's all topped of by the service, which is friendly and relaxed. To prolong the experience, there is an annex next door, in which you can purchase some of the freshly made items served in the dining room.

Familiar with Les Cailloux as clients, the directors naturally chose this charming restaurant for the scene of this romantic meeting.

LA CAVE LA BOURGOGNE

location for:

MUNICH

by STEVEN SPIELBERG

with ÉRIC BANA, DANIEL CRAIG, CIARÁN HINDS, MATHIEU KASSOVITZ,

HANNS ZISCHLER, AYELET ZURER, GEOFFREY RUSH

• 2006 •

*Michael Lonsdale and Mathieu Amalric
advise Éric Bana to discontinue his quest*

LA CAVE
LA BOURGOGNE
-
144, rue Mouffetard
75005 Paris
-
Ⓜ Censier-Daubenton
-
☎ 01 47 07 82 80
-
Price:
★★☆☆☆

WATCH THE TRAILER

La Cave la Bourgogne has been managed with passion and humility for twenty years by the same friendly owners. Its prime location has indulged it with a huge terrace, where you can enjoy simple, traditional food and delicious wines from small producers, without reservation.

On the day of shooting, Steven Spielberg cordoned off the area and had all anachronistic elements, such as cars and scooters, removed. Residents were not able to keep souvenirs as they were prohibited from taking photos.

SPECIAL THANKS TO

Eternal devotion to our fairy godmother Virginie, who swept away our doubts and hang-ups about the project.
Unwavering friendship to David, an exceptional mentor and Grand Master of the 'always better'.
Unconditional esteem to Constance, Florence, Bruno, Eryck, Pierre and Philippe, whose eyes always shone with encouragement. Constant comradeship to Stanislas, who enhanced our wishes beyond all our hopes.
A tip of the hat to Pierre-Olivier, who criss-crossed Paris on a bicycle to present us with the best shots.
Invaluable recognition to Séverine and Bruno, who opened the doors for us
to the fortified kingdom of publishing.
Heartfelt gratitude to Fabienne and Juliette for having made this dream possible with a big 'YES'.
Exclusive love to our Stars for their sweet patience as they watched us running about.
Infinite affection to our dear parents and their serene confidence in supporting
all our projects, even the wackiest ones.

CREDITS

• PAGE 8 *MARIE-ANTOINETTE*. 2006. Director: Sofia Coppola. Screenwriter: Sofia Coppola. Executive Producers: Francis Ford Coppola, Paul Rassam, Fred Roos, Matthew Tolmach. Producers: Sofia Coppola, Ross Katz. Co-producer: Callum Greene. Distribution: Pathé Distribution. Adapted from the novel *Marie-Antoinette*. Author: Antonia Fraser. • PAGE 10 *'QUARTIER DES ENFANTS ROUGES' – PARIS, I LOVE YOU*. 2006. Director: Olivier Assayas. Screenwriter: Olivier Assayas. Producers: Emmanuel Benbihy, Claudie Ossard. Distribution: La Fabrique de film. • PAGE 12 *THE STORY OF MY LIFE*. 2004. Director: Laurent Tirard.Screenwriters: Laurent Tirard, Grégoire Vigneron. Producers: Olivier Delbosc, Marc Missonnier. Distribution: EuropaCorp Distribution. • PAGE 14 *A HAPPY EVENT*. 2011. Director: Rémi Bezançon.Screenwriters: Rémi Bezançon, Vanessa Portal. Producers: Isabelle Grellat, Éric Altmayer, Nicolas Altmayer. Distribution: Gaumont Distribution. Adapted from the novel Un heureux événement. Author: Eliette Abecassis. • PAGE 15 *POLISSE*. 2011. Director: Maïwenn.Screenwriters: Maïwenn, Emmanuelle Bercot. Producteur : Alain Attal. Distribution: Mars Distribution. • PAGES 16, 50,160, 168, 184, 191 *MIDNIGHT IN PARIS*. 2011. Director: Woody Allen. Screenwriter: Woody Allen. Executive Producer: Javier Mendez. Producers: Letty Aronson, Jaume Roures, Stephen Tenenbaum. CoProducers: Raphaël Benoliel, Helen Robin. Distribution: Mars Distribution. • PAGE 18 *TELL NO ONE*. 2006. Director: Guillaume Canet.Screenwriters: Guillaume Canet, Philippe Lefebvre. Producteur : Alain Attal. Distribution: EuropaCorp Distribution. Adapted from the novel Tell no one. Author: Harlan Coben. • PAGE 22 *CHÉRI*. 2009. Director: Stephen Frears. Screenwriter: Christopher Hampton. Executive Producers: Simon Fawcett, Christopher Hampton, François Ivernel, Jessica Lange, Cameron McCracken. Producers: Thom Mount, Tracey Seaward, Bill Kenwright, Andras Hamori. Co-producer: Raphaël Benoliel. Distribution: Pathé Distribution. Adapted from the novel *Chéri*. Author: Colette. • PAGE 25 *THE ACTRESS' BALL*. 2009. Director: Maïwenn. Screenwriter: Maïwenn. Producers: François Kraus, Denis Pineau-Valencienne. Distribution: SND. • PAGE 26 *W.E*. 2012. Director: Madonna.Screenwriters: Madonna, Alek Keshishian. Executive Producers: Scott Franklin, Harvey Weinstein, Donna Gigliotti. Producers: Madonna, Kris Thykier. CoProducers: Sara Zambreno, Colin Vaines. Distribution: Pretty Pictures. • PAGE 28 *LA BOUM 2*. 1982. Director: Claude Pinoteau.Screenwriters: Danièle Thompson, Claude Pinoteau. Executive Producers: Gérard Croce, Marc Goldstaub. Producers: Marcel Dassault, Alain Poiré. Distribution: Gaumont. • PAGE 30 *THE BEAT THAT MY HEART SKIPPED*. 2005. Director: Jacques Audiard.Screenwriters: Jacques Audiard, Tonino Benacquista. Producteur : Pascal Caucheteux. Distribution: UGC. Remake du film : Mélodie pour un tueur, 1978. Director: James Toback. • PAGE 33 *THE BOURNE IDENTITY*. 2002. Director: Doug Liman.Screenwriters: Tony Gilroy, William Blake Herron. Executive Producers: Frank Marshall, Robert Ludlum. Producers: Doug Liman, Patrick Crowley, Richard N. Gladstein. Distribution: United International Pictures (UIP). Adapted from the novel The Bourne Identity. Author: Robert Ludlum. • PAGE 34 *THE CORSICAN FILE*. 2004. Director: Alain Berbérian.Screenwriters: Christian Clavier, Michel Delgado. Producteur : Alain Goldman. Producteur associé : Catherine Morisse-Monceau. Distribution: Gaumont Columbia Tristar Films. Adapté de la BD : L'Enquête corse. Author: Pétillon. • PAGE 36 *THE TOURIST*. 2010. Director: Florian Henckel von Donnersmarck.Screenwriters: Julian Fellowes, Christopher McQuarrie, Florian Henckel von Donnersmarck. Producers: Gary Barber, Roger Birnbaum, Jonathan Glickman, Tim Headington, Graham King. Co-producer: Denis O'Sullivan. Distribution: StudioCanal. Remake du film : Anthony Zimmer, 2005. Director: Jérôme Salle. • PAGES 38, 98 *PARIS*. 2008. Director: Cédric Klapisch. Screenwriter: Cédric Klapisch. Producteur : Bruno Levy. Distribution: Mars Distribution. • PAGE 40 *COCO BEFORE CHANEL*. 2009. Director: Anne Fontaine. Screenwriters: Anne Fontaine, Camille Fontaine, Christopher Hampton, Jacques Fieschi. Producers: Philippe Carcassonne, Caroline Benjo, Carole Scotta, Simon Arnal-Szlovak. Distribution: Warner Bros. France. Adapted from the novel L'Irrégulière. Author: Edmonde Charles-Roux. • PAGE 43 *SOMETHING'S GOTTA GIVE*. 2004. Director: Nancy Meyers. Screenwriter: Nancy Meyers. Producers: Nancy

Meyers, Bruce A. Block. Distribution: Warner Bros. France. • PAGE 44 *VATEL*. 2000. Director: Roland Joffé. Screenwriter: Jeanne Labrune. Producteur associé : Catherine Morisse-Monceau. Producers: Alain Goldman, Roland Joffé. Producteur délégué : Patrick Bordier. Co-producer: Timothy Burrill. Distribution: Gaumont Buena Vista International (GBVI). • PAGES 46, 150 *ROMANTICS ANONYMOUS*. 2010. Director: Jean-Pierre Améris.Screenwriters: Philippe Blasband, Jean-Pierre Améris. Producers: Nathalie Gastaldo, Philippe Godeau. Distribution: StudioCanal. • PAGE 53 *L'AVENTURE, C'EST L'AVENTURE*. 1972. Director: Claude Lelouch. Screenwriters: Claude Lelouch, Pierre Uytterhoeven. Producers: Georges Dancigers, Alexandre Mnouchkine. Distribution: Les films 13. • PAGE 54 *BREATHLESS*. 1960. Director: Jean-Luc Godard.Screenwriters: Jean-Luc Godard, François Truffaut. Producteur : Georges de Beauregard. Distribution: Les Acacias. • PAGE 56 *L'AMOUR C'EST MIEUX À DEUX*. 2010. Réalisateurs : Dominique Farrugia, Arnaud Lemort.Screenwriters: Arnaud Lemort, Franck Dubosc. Executive Producer: Dominique Brunner. Producteur délégué : Dominique Farrugia. Distribution: StudioCanal. • PAGES 58, 122 *LA FEMME NIKITA*. 1990. Director: Luc Besson. Screenwriter: Luc Besson. Executive Producers: Claude Besson, Jérôme Chalou. Producteur : Patrice Ledoux. CoProducers: Mario Cecchi Gori, Vittorio Cecchi Gori, Luc Besson. Distribution: Gaumont. • PAGE 60 *HÔTEL CHEVALIER* prologue to *THE DARJEELING LIMITED*. 2008. Director: Wes Anderson. Screenwriter: Wes Anderson. Executive Producer: Patrice Haddad. Producteur : Wes Anderson. Producteur délégué : Thierry Bettas-Bégalin. Producteur associé : Pierre Cléaud. Distribution: Twentieth Century Fox France. • PAGES 62, 97 *LITTLE WHITE LIES*. 2010. Director: Guillaume Canet. Screenwriter: Guillaume Canet. Executive Producer: Hugo Sélignac. Producteur : Alain Attal. Distribution: EuropaCorp Distribution. • PAGE 64 *THE DEVIL WEARS PRADA*. 2006. Director: David Frankel. Screenwriter: Aline Brosh McKenna. Executive Producers: Joseph M. Caracciolo Jr., Carla Hacken, Karen Rosenfelt. Producteur : Wendy Finerman. Distribution: Twentieth Century Fox France. Adapted from the novel The Devil Wears Prada. Author: Lauren Weisberger. • PAGES 66, 210 *HUNTING AND GATHERING*. 2007. Director: Claude Berri. Screenwriter: Claude Berri. Executive Producer: Pierre Grunstein. Producteur associé : Nathalie Rheims. Distribution: Pathé Distribution. Adapted from the novel Hunting and Gathering. Author: Anna Gavalda. • PAGES 68, 71 *AVENUE MONTAIGNE*. 2006. Director: Danièle Thompson.Screenwriters: Danièle Thompson, Christopher Thompson. Producers: Christine Gozlan, Alain Sarde. Distribution: Mars Distribution. • PAGES 72, 101, 102, 190 *CHANGE OF PLANS*. 2009. Director: Danièle Thompson.Screenwriters: Danièle Thompson, Christopher Thompson. Executive Producer: David Poirot. Producers: Alain Terzian, Christine Gozlan. Distribution: StudioCanal. • PAGE 74 *A VIEW TO A KILL*. 1985. Director: John Glen.Screenwriters: Richard Maibaum, Michael G. Wilson. Producers: Albert R. Broccoli, Michael G. Wilson. Distribution: United International Pictures (UIP). Adapted from the short story A View to Kill. Author: Ian Fleming. • PAGE 76 *THE BIG PICTURE*. 2010. Director: Éric Lartigau.Screenwriters: Éric Lartigau, Laurent de Bartillat. Producteur : Pierre-Ange Le Pogam. Distribution: EuropaCorp Distribution. Adapted from the novel L'homme qui voulait vivre sa vie. Author: Douglas Kennedy. • PAGE 80 *OSS 117 : CAIRO, NEST OF SPIES*. 2006. Director: Michel Hazanavicius.Screenwriters: Jean-François Halin, Michel Hazanavicius. Executive Producer: Sarim Fassi-Fihri. Producers: Éric Altmayer, Nicolas Altmayer. Associate Producers: Patrick Quinet, Gaetan David, André Logie. Distribution: Gaumont Columbia Tristar Films. Adapted from the OSS 117 novels. Author: Jean Bruce. • PAGE 83 *HÔTEL DU NORD*. 1938. Director: Marcel Carné.Screenwriters: Henri Jeanson, Jean Aurenche. Producers: Jean Lévy-Strauss, Onésime Grinkrug, Joseph Lucachevitch. Distribution: Cocinor. Adapted from the novel Hôtel du Nord. Author: Eugène Dabit. • PAGE 84 *RUSSIAN DOLLS*. 2005. Director: Cédric Klapisch.Screenwriters: Cédric Klapisch, Barbara Constantine. Producers: Bruno Levy, Matthew Justice. Distribution: Mars Distribution. • PAGES 86, 194 *'LOLITA' – THE PLAYERS*. 2012. Director: Éric Lartigau.Screenwriters: Jean Dujardin, Gilles Lellouche, Stéphane Joly, Nicolas Bedos, Philippe Caverivière. Producers: Jean

Dujardin, Éric Hannezo, Guillaume Lacroix. Distribution: Mars Distribution. • PAGE 88, 141, 142 *BELOVED*. 2011. Director: Christophe Honoré. Screenwriter: Christophe Honoré. Producteur : Pascal Caucheteux. Distribution: Le Pacte. • PAGE 89 *LOVE SONGS*. 2007. Director: Christophe Honoré. Screenwriter: Christophe Honoré. Producteur : Paulo Branco. Distribution: Bac Films. • PAGE 91 *FRANTIC*. 1988. Director: Roman Polanski.Screenwriters: Roman Polanski, Gérard Brach, Robert Towne, Jeff Gross. Producers: Tim Hampton, Thom Mount. Distribution: Warner Bros. France. • PAGE 92 *LA VIE EN ROSE*. 2007. Director: Olivier Dahan. Screenwriter: Olivier Dahan. Producteur : Alain Goldman. Distribution: TFM Distribution. • PAGE 106 *THE CONCERT*. 2009. Director: Radu Mihaileanu.Screenwriters: Matthew Robbins, Radu Mihaileanu, Alain-Michel Blanc, Hector Cabello Reyes, Thierry Degrandi, Hector Cabello Reyes, Thierry Degrandi. Producteur : Alain Attal. Distribution: EuropaCorp Distribution. • PAGES 108, 113 *WHEN THE CAT'S AWAY*. 1996. Director: Cédric Klapisch. Screenwriter: Cédric Klapisch. Producers: Aïssa Djabri, Farid Lahouassa, Manuel Munz. Distribution: Bac Films. • PAGES 114, 202 *BEFORE SUNSET*. 2005. Director: Richard Linklater.Screenwriters: Richard Linklater, Ethan Hawke, Julie Delpy, Kim Krizan. Executive Producer: John Sloss. Producers: Anne Walker-McBay, Richard Linklater. Co-producer: Isabelle Coulet. Distribution: CTV International. • PAGE 116 *I'VE BEEN WAITING SO LONG*. 2004. Director: Thierry Klifa.Screenwriters: Thierry Klifa, Christopher Thompson. Producers: François Kraus, Denis Pineau-Valencienne. Distribution: Mars Distribution. • PAGE 118, *LE PÈRE NOËL EST UNE ORDURE*. 1982. Director: Jean-Marie Poiré. Screenwriters: Josiane Balasko, Marie-Anne Chazel, Christian Clavier, Gérard Jugnot, Thierry Lhermitte, Bruno Moynot, Jean-Marie Poiré. Producteur : Yves Rousset-Rouard. Executive Producer: Christian Ferry. Distribution: Compagnie Commerciale Française Cinématographique (CCFC), GEF. • PAGE 121 *'BASTILLE' – PARIS, I LOVE YOU*. 2006. Director: Isabel Coixet. Screenwriter: Isabel Coixet. Producers: Emmanuel Benbihy, Claudie Ossard. Distribution: La Fabrique de film. • PAGE 128 *ITINÉRAIRE D'UN ENFANT GÂTÉ*. 1988. Director: Claude Lelouch. Screenwriter: Claude Lelouch. Executive Producers: Tania Zazulinsky, Claude Albouze. Producers: Jean-Paul Belmondo, Claude Lelouch. Co-producer: Gerhard Schmidt. Distribution: Les Films 13. • PAGES 129, 217 *A MONSTER IN PARIS*. 2011. Director: Éric Bergeron.Screenwriters: Stéphane Kazandjian, Éric Bergeron. Executive Producers: Nadia Khamlich, Adrian Politowski, Gilles Waterkeyn. Producteur : Luc Besson. Producteur associé : Rémi Burah. Distribution: EuropaCorp Distribution. • PAGES 126, 130, 133, 214 *AMÉLIE*. 2001. Director: Jean-Pierre Jeunet.Screenwriters: Jean-Pierre Jeunet, Guillaume Laurant. Executive Producer: Claudie Ossard. Producers: Jean-Marc Deschamps, Claudie Ossard. Co-producer: Helmut Breuer. Distribution: UFD. • PAGE 134 *MOULIN ROUGE!* 2001. Director: Baz Luhrmann. Screenwriters: Baz Luhrmann, Craig Pearce. Producers: Fred Baron, Martin Brown, Baz Luhrmann. Co-producer: Catherine Knapman. Producteurs associés : Steve E. Andrews, Catherine Martin. Distribution: UFD. • PAGE 135 *JULIE & JULIA*. 2009. Director: Nora Ephron. Screenwriter: Nora Ephron. Producers: Nora Ephron, Laurence Mark, Amy Robinson, Éric Steel. Producteur associé : J.J. Sacha. Co-producer: Dianne Dreyer. Distribution: Sony Pictures Releasing France. Adapted from the novel My Year of Cooking Dangerously. Author: Julie Powell. Adapted from the novel My life in Paris. Auteur : Julia Child, Alex Prud'homme. • PAGES 162, 172, 182 *THE INTOUCHABLES*. 2011. Réalisateurs : Éric Toledano, Olivier Nakache.Screenwriters: Éric Toledano, Olivier Nakache. Producers: Nicolas Duval, Yann Zenou, Laurent Zeitoun. Distribution: Gaumont Distribution. Adapted from the novel A Second Wind. Author: Philippe Pozzo di Borgo. • PAGE 137 *INGLOURIOUS BASTERDS*. 2009. Director: Quentin Tarantino. Screenwriter: Quentin Tarantino. Executive Producers: Harvey Weinstein, Bob Weinstein, Érica Steinberg, Lloyd Phillips. Producteur : Lawrence Bender. Producteurs associés : Pilar Savone, Bruce Moriarty, William Paul Clark. CoProducers: Charlie Woebcken, Christoph Fisser, Henning Molfenter. Distribution: Universal Pictures International France. • PAGE 138 *DÉPRESSION ET DES POTES*. 2012. Director: Arnaud Lemort. Screenwriter: Arnaud Lemort. Executive Producer: Dominique Brunner. Producteur délégué : Dominique Farrugia. Distribution: StudioCanal. • PAGE 142 *TAKEN*. 2008. Director: Pierre Morel. Screenwriters: Robert Mark Kamen, Luc Besson, Karl Gajdusek. Executive Producer:

Didier Hoarau. Producers: Luc Besson, India Osborne, Pierre-Ange Le Pogam, Irwin Winkler, Jill Cutler. Distribution: EuropaCorp Distribution. • PAGES 146, 174 *LOVE LASTS THREE YEARS*. 2012. Director: Frédéric Beigbeder.Screenwriters: Frédéric Beigbeder, Christophe Turpin, Gilles Verdiani. Producers: Michaël Gentile, Alain Kruger. Producteur associé : Lauraine Heftler. Distribution: EuropaCorp Distribution. Adapted from the novel L'amour dure trois ans. Author: Frédéric Beigbeder. • PAGE 148 *MENSCH*. 2009. Director: Steve Suissa.Screenwriters: Steve Suissa, Stéphane Cabel. Producteurs délégués : Laurent Pétin, Michèle Pétin. Distribution: ARP Sélection. • PAGE 153 *A VERY LONG ENGAGEMENT*. 2004. Director: Jean-Pierre Jeunet.Screenwriters: Guillaume Laurant, Jean-Pierre Jeunet. Executive Producer: Bill Gerber. Producteur associé : Francis Boespflug. Distribution: Warner Bros. France. Adapted from the novel Un long dimanche de fiançailles. Author: Sébastien Japrisot. • PAGE 154, 192 *HUGO*. 2011. Director: Martin Scorsese. Screenwriter: John Logan. Executive Producers: Christi Dembrowski, Georgia Kacandes, Emma Tillinger, David Crockett. Producers: Graham King, Johnny Depp, Tim Headington, Martin Scorsese. Distribution: Metropolitan FilmExport. Adapted from the novel The Invention of Hugo Cabret. Author: Brian Selznick. • PAGE 156 *HEREAFTER*. 2011. Director: Clint Eastwood. Screenwriter: Peter Morgan. Producers: Kathleen Kennedy, Clint Eastwood, Robert Lorenz. Distribution: Warner Bros. France. • PAGES 166, 167, 206 *GAINSBOURG: A HEROIC LIFE*. 2010. Director: Joann Sfar. Screenwriter: Joann Sfar. Producers: Didier Lupfer, Marc Du Pontavice. Distribution: Universal Pictures International France. • PAGE 176 *TANGUY*. 2001. Director: Étienne Chatiliez.Screenwriters: Laurent Chouchan, Étienne Chatiliez. Producteur : Charles Gassot. Distribution: UFD. • PAGE 178 *THE DISCREET*. 1990. Director: Christian Vincent.Screenwriters: Christian Vincent, Jean-Pierre Ronssin. Producers: Alain Rocca, Adeline Lecallier. Distribution: Mars Distribution. • PAGE 179 *THE DA VINCI CODE*. 2006. Director: Ron Howard. Screenwriter: Akiva Goldsman. Executive Producers: Dan Brown, Todd Hallowell. Producers: Brian Grazer, John Calley. CoProducers: Louisa Velis, Kathleen McGill. Distribution: Gaumont Columbia Tristar Films. Adapted from the novel Da Vinci Code. Author: Dan Brown. • PAGE 187 *2 DAYS IN PARIS*. 2007. Director: Julie Delpy. Screenwriter: Julie Delpy. Executive Producer: Charles Favrol. Producers: Julie Delpy, Christophe Mazodier, Thierry Potok. CoProducers: Ulf Israel, Werner Wirsing. Producteurs associés : Nikolaus Lohmann, Tilo Seiffert, Hubert Toint. Distribution: Rezo Films. • PAGE 188 *CONVERSATIONS WITH MY GARDENER*. 2007. Director: Jean Becker.Screenwriters: Jean Becker, Jean Cosmos, Jacques Monnet. Producteur délégué : Louis Becker. Distribution: StudioCanal. Adapted from the novel Dialogue avec mon jardinier. Author: Henri Cueco. • PAGE 197 *LE PÉRIL JEUNE*. 1995. Director: Cédric Klapisch.Screenwriters: Cédric Klapisch, Santiago Amigorena, Alexis Galmot, Daniel Thieux. Producers: Aïssa Djabri, Farid Lahouassa. Distribution: Gaumont Buena Vista International (GBVI). • PAGE 200 *THREE COLOURS: BLUE*. 1993. Director: Krzysztof Kieslowski.Screenwriters: Krzysztof Kieslowski, Krzysztof Piesiewicz, Agnieszka Holland, Slawomir Holland, Edward Zebrowski. Producteur : Marin Karmitz. Distribution: MKL. • PAGE 204 *HAPPINESS NEVER COMES ALONE*. 2012. Director: James Huth.Screenwriters: James Huth, Sonja Shillito. Executive Producers: Sonja Shillito, Frédéric Doniguian. Producteur : Richard Grandpierre. Distribution: Pathé Distribution. • PAGE 212 *SAGAN*. 2008. Director: Diane Kurys. Screenwriters: Diane Kurys, Martine Moriconi, Claire LeMaréchal. Producteur : Diane Kurys. Distribution: EuropaCorp Distribution. • PAGE 216 *JULES AND JIM*. 1962. Director: François Truffaut.Screenwriters: François Truffaut, Jean Gruault. Producteur : Marcel Berbert. Distribution: Cinédis. Adapted from the novel Jules et Jim. Author: Henri-Pierre Roché. • PAGE 218 *DELICACY*. 2011. Réalisateurs : David Foenkinos, Stéphane Foenkinos. Screenwriter: David Foenkinos. Producers: Marc-Antoine Robert, Xavier Rigault. Distribution: StudioCanal. Adapted from the novel La Délicatesse. Author: David Foenkinos. • PAGE 220 *MUNICH*. 2006. Director: Steven Spielberg.Screenwriters: Éric Roth, Tony Kushner. Producers: Steven Spielberg, Kathleen Kennedy, Barry Mendel, Colin Wilson. Distribution: United International Pictures (UIP). Adapted from the book Vengeance: The True Story of an Israeli Counter-Terrorist Team. Author: George Jonas.

Authors: Barbara Boespflug and Beatrice Billon
Photos: Pierre-Olivier Signe
Art Direction and Design: Stanislas Potié – Gr8! Design

Translation from French: Anne McDowall
Editing-Proofreading: Lyn Thompson Lemaire

Direction: Fabienne Kriegel
Editorial Manager: Juliette de Lavaur
Assistant Editor: Françoise Mathay, assisted by Marion Dellapina
Proofreading: La Machine à mots
Production: Marion Lance
Photoengraving: Quat'coul
Partnerships and Direct Sales: Claire Le Cocguen (clecocguen@hachette-livre.fr)
Public Relations: Hélène Maurice (hmaurice@hachette-livre.fr)

First Published in French by
Éditions du Chêne – Hachette Livre, 2012
Original title : Paris fait son cinéma
© Éditions du Chêne – Hachette Livre, 2013
www.editionsduchene.fr

Published by Éditions du Chêne
(43, quai de Grenelle, 75905 Paris cedex 15)
Printed by Estella Graficas in Spain
Coypright Registration: July 2013
ISBN 978-2-81230-841-3
32/3743/5-01